UNMASKING ANNE FRANK

Her Famous Diary Exposed as a Literary Fraud

UNMASKING ANNE FRANK

Her Famous Diary Exposed as a Literary Fraud

IKUO SUZUKI

With Commentary By

KARL HAEMERS

Clemens & Blair, LLC

— 2022 —

CLEMENS & BLAIR, LLC

Text copyright © 2022, by Ikuo Suzuki
Introduction and Postscript © 2022, by Karl Haemers
Edited by Thomas Dalton

Clemens & Blair, LLC, is a non-profit educational publisher.
www.clemensandblair.com

Library of Congress Cataloging-in-Publication Data

Suzuki, Ikuo
Unmasking Anne Frank: Her Famous Diary Exposed as a Literary Fraud

p. cm.
Includes bibliographical references

ISBN 978-1737-4461-94
(pbk.: alk. paper)

1. Anne Frank 2. Holocaust

Printing number: 9 8 7 6 5 4 3 2 1

Printed in the United States of America on acid-free paper.

PRELIMINARY REMARKS

The Diary of Anne Frank—hereafter referred to as the 'Diary' or 'Anne's Diary'—is an international bestseller that needs no explanation. It is arguably one of the most widely known books in the world. It is also said that Japan is the country where it sold the most and was loved the most. Even today, Anne's Diary is one of the recommended books in Japanese elementary school book report assignments. However, there have been whisperings of forgery allegations about this work since shortly after the first Dutch version was published in 1947. In the Holocaust controversy, which is my original research theme, the allegations about this work have often been mentioned.

However, the Holocaust controversy and Anne's diary controversy are theoretically completely different. Surprisingly, Holocaust skeptics, generally called 'revisionists,' have paid little attention to the Diary—except for Professor Robert Faurisson, discussed in the main text. I, too, was completely ignorant of this issue, knowing only a few bits and pieces of information. When Mr. Sawaguchi asked me to write this book, to be honest, I was not very enthusiastic. However, as I gathered more information, it became clear that the controversy was far more complex than I had thought; it hid a very deep darkness I hope readers will relive my surprise and excitement as I entered the labyrinth of Anne's Diary. We know that, in general, behind that which is widely established and regarded as unquestionably true is often a deeper, unknown truth. Surely, Anne's Diary is one such example. I am satisfied if this work can help readers to realize the importance of being rightly skeptical about such things.

When reading this book, I recommend that you have the full Diary text at hand; this will deepen your understanding.

— Ikuo Suzuki

CONTENTS

FOREWORD
THOMAS DALTON

The following text was written by Japanese Holocaust researcher Ikuo Suzuki, a man who has spent many years critically examining the events of World War Two and specifically the details of the Jewish Holocaust. He also provided the initial rough English translation. Final editing of the full English text was performed by Karl Haemers, who also contributed the Introduction and an extended Postscript.

Though not directly related, the Anne Frank story and her famous diary are clearly an important part of the larger Holocaust narrative. In one sense, Anne—and her mother and sister—were simply three more victims of a German policy of isolating, excluding, and deporting European Jews. And yet, thanks to her diary, Anne's story is now a central element in the global education—or global indoctrination, some might say—on the suffering of the many Jewish Holocaust victims. Anne's diary does something special: it makes the suffering *individual*, and *personal*; its purpose is to make non-Jews feel her pain, and indeed the pain of all Jews who suffered at that time. The book today is targeted primarily at school-age children and teens, many of whom are now compelled to read at least portions of the diary as part of their public education. As such, the book is designed to build sympathy toward Jews, antipathy towards Nazi Germany (and indeed all Germans), and to vividly portray Jewish suffering. In this way, Gentile youth are presumed to be somewhat "inoculated" against the "disease" of anti-Semitism.

But what if Anne's famous diary is not what it seems? What if there are profound difficulties and unexplained issues regarding her writing? What if a number of absurdities and logical inconsistencies could be found, such that the whole context of the diary were thrown into doubt? Indeed, what if Anne never even wrote the famous diary that so many children read today? What if the diary was more of a novel, a literary construction, than an actual record of the daily personal life of a 13- or

14-year-old girl[1] living in wartime Amsterdam? In that case, we would have a major controversy on our hands. In such a case, we would have to admit that millions of schoolchildren have been fed a false, or at least misleading, story of Jewish suffering. And the, now, 30 million copies of the diary that have been sold worldwide[2] would have to be reconceived as fiction, and Anne's diary would be revealed as perhaps the most infamous instance of literary fraud in modern history.

In fact, the consequences of this discovery would be monumental. Researchers and educators around the world would be exposed as accomplices in a massive literary deception. The general public would then begin to wonder how such a gigantic fraud could ever come about, and worse—what other such frauds might be out there. Worst of all—for the global Jewish Lobby—people everywhere might come to doubt the traditional details of the entire Holocaust story. People everywhere might begin to ask some pertinent questions: Did 6 million Jews really die over the course of World War Two?[3] Did those infamous gas chambers at Auschwitz, Treblinka, and the other camps really work like we were told? Did Hitler ever really intend to literally kill all those Jews? And: What role did Jews play in causing World War Two in the first place?[4] If people start to ask these questions, the whole foundation of contemporary attitudes toward Jews could be overturned. People everywhere might begin to see Jews as, God forbid, liars and deceivers, as manipulators and exploiters, acting only in their own self-interest—a tragic outcome, to be sure.

---

[1] Anne was indeed 15 for two months of the diary period, out of 26 total months, or about 7% of the time. For 93% of the time, she was 13 or 14, hence my emphasis on those ages. We must constantly recall how young she was, and compare this to the words attributed to her.

[2] According to the US Holocaust Memorial Museum (accessed 1 July 2022).

[3] If 6 million died over a period of 68 months, or about 2,000 days, then an average of 3,000 Jews must have died every day, seven days a week, for the entire duration of the war. And these same 3,000 bodies must have been disposed of—burned or buried—on average, every day. A truly remarkable feat, if true.

[4] For details on these questions and others, see my books *Debating the Holocaust: A New Look at Both Sides* (4th ed., 2020) and *The Jewish Hand in the World Wars* (2019).

Suzuki is not the first to raise these troublesome issues. Already back in the late 1950s, Scandinavian skeptics were challenging the basics of the diary story. Then in 1958, a German high school teacher, Lothar Stielau, published a review of a play, *Tom Sawyer*, that included a single objectional sentence. He remarked, in passing, on "the forged diaries" of Eva Braun, the Queen of England, "and the hardly more authentic one of Anne Frank"; these fakes "earned several millions for the profiteers from Germany's defeat [in WW2]," said Stielau. For this minor indiscretion, he was drawn into a protracted lawsuit by Otto Frank and his Jewish lawyers, which ended in a whimper after three long years.[5] Then a few years later, in 1967, the writer Teressa Hendry published a skeptical article in *American Mercury* in which she named the Jew Meyer Levin as the true author of the diary—a claim that accords with our present writer Suzuki, as we will see. In 1975, Holocaust skeptic Richard Harwood argued against the diary's authenticity, as did British historian David Irving.[6]

The first substantial critique came in 1978, with the book *Anne Frank Diary—A Hoax?* by Ditlieb Felderer. This work is briefly examined below in the Introduction. Also in 1978, a professor of literature at the University of Lyon (France), Robert Faurisson, wrote an expert opinion for a legal case in which he laid out many absurdities and contradictions with the diary, as well as presenting a summary of his highly-revealing personal interview with Otto Frank. Faurisson's report—in fact, an extended essay—was published in French in 1980, as an English article ("Is the diary of Anne Frank genuine?") in 1982,[7] and in booklet form in 1985. But in the intervening 40 years, little more has appeared, until now.

In the present work, Suzuki provides a much-needed and scholarly update of the case for a fraudulent diary. Our present writers have the advantage of developments in the Anne Frank story over the past four

---

[5] A minor settlement was reached with Otto in late 1961, in which Stielau issued a retraction and agreed to pay 1,000 DM.

[6] Irving wrote, "Many forgeries are on record, as for instance that of the Diary of Anne Frank." He added that a legal suit by Meyer Levin against Otto Frank proved that both men were collaborators in the project.

[7] Available here: http://www.ihr.org//jhr/v03/v03index.html.

decades, including the discovery of new diary pages and the publication of such "authoritative" works as *The Diary of Anne Frank: The Critical Edition* (1989) and its follow-up, *The Revised Critical Edition* (2003). Books and videos are continuing to appear on a regular basis; since the year 2000, the database WorldCat indicates over 800 English-language releases on Anne Frank, or about 35 per year. Clearly the topic is very important, at least for certain people.

To properly grasp the nature of the literary fraud that is Anne Frank's diary, we need to review some of the essentials of Anne's story. So let's start there.

The Essentials of the Story

Anne Frank was born Annelies Marie Frank, in Frankfurt, Germany, on 12 June 1929. She was the youngest of the two Frank girls, her older sister Margot having been born in 1926. Anne's parents, Otto and Edith, lived a fairly conventional middle-class life in Frankfurt—Otto was a small businessman—until the rise of Adolf Hitler's National Socialist party in 1933, at which time they decided to flee to the Netherlands. Anne moved to Amsterdam in February 1934 when she was four years old. There she attended school, becoming quite fluent in Dutch, which became the primary language of the Frank family. Germany invaded the Netherlands in May 1940, putting new pressure on Dutch Jews, all of whom now had to adopt a low-profile existence. Eventually, the Frank family, along with another Jewish family of three and a dentist, went into hiding in an "annex" of her father's office building in central Amsterdam. They lived in hiding for around two years.

Sometime in mid-1944, perhaps early August, the Frank family was apprehended and deported to the Westerbork labor camp, and soon thereafter on to Auschwitz in the south of present-day Poland. At Auschwitz, Otto was separated from the three female members of his family; he would stay in the camp until its liberation, but the two Frank girls were shipped on to Bergen-Belsen labor camp in October 1944. (Edith died in Auschwitz.) Like many camps late in the war, Bergen-Belsen had a large outbreak of typhus; apparently both girls contracted the disease and died in February or March 1945. Anne's body was never found. She was 15 years old.

Unfortunately, these few sketchy details are about all that we can say with certainty about Anne/Annelies Frank. Everything else that we think we know about her is in doubt: what she wrote, how much she wrote, what she did during her 10 years in Amsterdam, what life was like during her two-year "hideout" in the annex of her father's office building, and so on. Most importantly, we literally do not know how much, if any, of the famous diary was written by her. And if Annelies was not the author of the diary—then who was? When did they write it? And why? These are a few of the critical questions that we will examine in the text to follow.

I will leave the detailed critique to our authors. Here, I simply want to review the conventional orthodoxy on the diary; even the standard account has so many bizarre twists and turns that one can hardly avoid the feeling that "something is up."

Anne allegedly received her first diary book—a red and white checked notebook that she herself picked out—on her 13th birthday, 12 June 1942. She made some cursory notes in it that day, and then began her first official entry on 14 June. Entries were made, sometimes daily, sometimes weekly, sometimes less often. The final entry came on 1 August 1944, three days before the family was allegedly arrested on 4 August.

The first odd fact is that Anne allegedly wrote not one, but two diaries—or rather, two copies of the same events. Following the conventional notation, I will refer to these as the "A" and "B" versions.[8] The A-version is the original, and we might say, authentic diary—presuming that such a thing exists. This was the version that Anne wrote as events happened, first, in her red-and-white checked book, and then later in two other books. The A-version is the *only* one that ordinary people would consider a legitimate diary—entries written by hand, by the (alleged) author, at the time that things actually happened.

---

[8] For some reason, the traditionalists use lower-case 'a' and 'b'; but this is more confusing to read and cite. Perhaps it was intended this way. Suzuki often refers to the "diary" and "edited" versions, respectively.

The red-and-white checked book sufficed for Anne until 5 Dec 1942, or about six months. It covers the time before hiding, which began on 6 July 1942, and about five months afterward. Then the entries stop, even though the booklet had remaining blank pages; the reasons for this are unknown.

Then there is a large gap in the A-version. Presumably Anne continued to write in another book, or books, but these have been lost. The gap runs for over a year: from 5 Dec 1942 to 22 Dec 1943. For this entire period, we have no "original" (A-version) entries at all. Then on 22 Dec 1943, she began writing in a "school notebook" or "exercise book"—which survived the war, even though, oddly, one cannot find a photograph of this notebook (exterior). This book #2 sufficed until 17 April 1944—just four months—when Anne switched to a third notebook, which also cannot be found in a photograph, that ran until the final entry in August 1944.

Hence, the authentic, A-version covers three physical books, but has a full year gap—virtually all of 1943. The three books survived the war; the red-checked book is on display at the Anne Frank House, but the other two notebooks are kept out of sight, for some reason.

Then, as the story goes, in May 1944, Anne decided to "rewrite" her entire diary. Beginning on 20 May, and even as she was writing in the 3rd book of her A-version, Anne simultaneously began a "B-version" of the diary. She went back to the very beginning, June 1942, and rewrote the diary—the *entire* diary—on a series of "loose sheets" of paper. Miraculously, all of the "loose sheets" survived the war—at least, up to the date 29 Mar 1944, at which time they stop; presumably that was as far as Anne got when the family was arrested.

Luckily, the B-version loose sheets cover the year 1943—the very year that A is missing. Thus, in a sense, we do have the "entire" diary: A + B for about half of the time, and B-only for the other half. All this is depicted on the timeline in Figure 1.

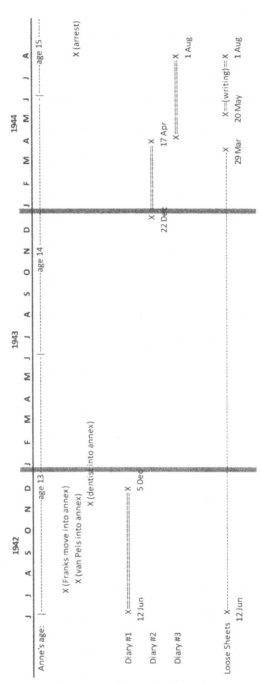

Figure 1: Diary timeline

The Novelized B-Version

Allegedly, Anne undertook the B-version rewrite because she wanted to publish her diary after the war. A Dutch radio broadcast of 28 Mar 1944 called for people to save their personal letters and diaries as a record of their wartime experiences. The next day Anne wrote about this broadcast, saying "they all made a rush at my diary" (who 'they' are is unexplained). She added, "Just imagine how interesting it would be if I were to publish a romance of the *Secret Annex*, the title alone would be enough to make people think it was a detective story" (A-version). In the standard, "definitive" version of the diary that people actually read (neither 'A' nor 'B,' as I will explain), it reads, "… if I were to publish a <u>novel</u> about the Secret Annex".[9] Evidently, then, Anne had in mind a novelized version of her diary. This new, B-version was begun, she says, by 20 May (as noted above).

In the rewrite, Anne made many changes. As we read in the *Revised Critical Edition* of 2003:

> She changed, rearranged, sometimes combined entries of various dates, expanded and abbreviated. In addition she drew up a list of name changes. (p. 61)

The van Pels family of three that were in hiding with Anne became the "van Daan" family; the dentist Pfeffer became "Dussel," and so on. The changes are extensive, to put it mildly. Fortunately, in the *Revised Critical Edition* (RCE), we can directly compare the 'A' and 'B' versions, side by side—except of course for 1943, for which there is no A-version at all, and for post-29 Mar 1944, for which there is no B-version. For the roughly nine months where we have both versions, one can scarcely find a date without major changes; in some cases, the B-entry is deleted, and in some cases, a B-date is invented when there was no A entry in the first place. Anne was indeed novelizing her diary.

---

[9] *The Diary of a Young Girl* (Doubleday, 1991/2001), p. 245.

Enter Otto

After the arrest, deportation of the family to Auschwitz, and Anne's subsequent transfer to Bergen-Belsen, Otto was freed from Auschwitz, having spent some five months there—without being "exterminated".[10] The war in Europe ended in May, and by early June, her father Otto had worked his way back to Amsterdam. He sought out a former female employee of his, Miep Gies, who had assisted their 'hideout' for the two years. By sheer luck, Miep, along with another female Dutch co-worker, Bep Voskuijl, had returned to the hideout later in the day of the arrest and, in one version of the story, found Anne's diaries and loose sheets strewn about on the floor. Miep collected the writings and stored them away, returning them to Otto in July 1945.

Upon reading the diaries, Otto immediately decided to type them up—at least, "the essentials"—in order to pass along to "relatives and friends".[11] We may call this version "Typescript 0," to follow in the orthodox notation. Sadly, "this first copy was lost." So Otto began to type out another version, now known as "Typescript I," drawing on both the diary books and the loose sheets. Along the way, he exercised considerable editorial discretion; he "typed out those items he wanted to use, cut some out, and then joined them up." He also "omitted some rather duller entries" and other "certain passages."

Yet Otto was evidently unhappy with this edition, and so he sent a copy of TS1 to a friend, Albert Cauvern, a journalist and "dramatist." Cauvern proceeded to significantly mark up the text: "numerous changes and improvements," "changes of proper names," and, ominously, some "amplifications." Yet other passages were deleted.

Cauvern's hand-marked edits are still extant. But, oddly, another version of TS1 that exists has hand-marked corrections that are *not* those of Cauvern; apparently another, unknown person also made edits to TS1.

---

[10] Auschwitz was "liberated" by the Soviet army on 27 January 1945. This was a month or so before Anne died in Bergen-Belsen.
[11] As reported in RCE, p. 62.

In January 1946, the edited version(s) of TS1 were typed up, and this new typed edition came to be known as "Typescript II" (TS2).

TS2 was circulated among "friends and close acquaintances," including Kurt Baschwitz, Werner Cahn, and an encyclopedia editor named Jan Romein. These friends actively sought out publishers for the book, but with no success. Romein then published a small article about the diary on 3 April 1946. Oddly, the article never mentions Anne by name; instead we read of "a child's voice," "this Jewish girl," etc. The text of the diary, he said, was incredibly mature: "she showed an insight into the failings of human nature so infallible that it would have astonished one in an adult, let alone in a child".[12] Here we must recall that we are discussing a 13/14-year-old girl (and, for two months, 15). Unless she was a super-genius—and contemporaneous evidence suggests otherwise—then the maturity of the text alone should cause us to suspect some judicious editing at work, if not total fabrication. If the writing of a mature adult allegedly appears in the mouth of a 13-year-old girl, especially a dead one, we ought to be highly suspicious.

In any case, Romein's little article garnered much attention and drew in a number of prospective publishers. One was "Contact," a local Dutch publishing house. The RCE describes the lengthy negotiation process, but in the end, Contact was selected as the publisher of choice. They started with TS2, and then began to make their own rounds of edits. Altered were "typing errors," stylistic changes to match "house rules," "choice of words," and so on. There were yet more deletions and "amplifications." In the end, says the RCE, "the reader was left with a literary work by Anne Frank rather than with an autobiographical document *sensu strictu* ['strictly speaking']" (p. 71). This is a highly damning admission. In other, more honest words, what they had produced was a literary construction, not the actual diary of a 13/14-year-old girl. To then pass off the document as "Anne's diary" amounts to literary fraud, by any measure of the term.

In this way, *Het Achterhuis*—literally, 'the Back House'—was published in Dutch, in the summer of 1947.

---

[12] RCE, p. 68.

In parallel to all this, Otto had arranged for a copy of TS2 to be translated into German, via the efforts of an elderly acquaintance of his, Anneliese Schütz. In the process, she exercised yet more editorial license, to a degree greater than anyone had thus far. Eventually this "translation" (if one may use the word) was published, in 1950, as *Das Tagebuch der Anne Frank*.

Also in 1950, a Mrs. B. Mooyaart-Doubleday was enlisted to translate *Het Achterhuis* into English. Today this is known as the "C" version; it also appears in the 2003 RCE book, in parallel with A and B versions. Thus, the RCE, which runs to 850 numbered pages, contains fully *three versions* of the diary: the original (A), Anne's loose-sheet rewrite (B), and the Mooyaart translation of TS2 (C)—all side-by-side. The reader will be excused if his head is spinning at this point, given the convoluted history of "the" diary of Anne Frank.

As if this weren't bad enough, the "definitive" English edition of the diary—*The Diary of a Young Girl*, published by Doubleday in 1991—is yet different from A, B, and C. This version, the one that the public actually reads today, is "edited by Otto Frank and Mirjam Pressler," and "translated by Susan Massotty." One might be tempted to call this the "D-version" of the diary, but apparently the powers that be have decided that this would unduly complicate matters.

"Comes a Showman"

Next we come to the character Meyer Levin (1905-1981). A Jewish-American journalist and novelist from Chicago, Meyer had a long and intriguing career—first as an editor and film critic for *Esquire* magazine and later as a reporter on the Spanish Civil War. As Suzuki explains, before WW2 Levin began working for the US defense department, specifically as a propagandist in the Psychological Warfare Division. He also published a small book in late 1946 or early 1947 titled *Kibbutz Buchenwald*, which was allegedly a translation of a diary of the members of a Kibbutz near that infamous camp. This marks Levin as a man interested in wartime diaries, especially when they might serve a propagandistic or ideological purpose.

On the official view (as in RCE, pp. 78-82), Levin doesn't appear on the scene until November 1950, when he "eulogizes" Anne's diary in a journal of the American Jewish Congress. At some point in time, he makes acquaintances with Otto Frank, and in March 1952, Otto appoints Levin as his "literary agent" in the US. Obviously such a thing does not happen without a long period of personal contact and working experience.

To summarize RCE's sanitized version of the Levin story: From June 1951, we learn that Levin wants badly to write and produce a play about Anne. He signs a contract with Otto in November of that year, in the hope of finding a producer willing to take on Levin's project. He fails. In October of 1953, Otto grants rights to another Jewish producer, Kermit Bloomgarden, who immediately asked screenwriters Albert Hackett and Frances Goodrich to write a "dramatized version" of the diary. The play premiered in October 1955, to great success. Levin, of course, was infuriated, and he sued Bloomgarden and Otto in late 1956 for plagiarism and breach of contract. The former charge eventually went to a jury, who found in Levin's favor and awarded him $50,000 in damages in January 1958. But the award was overturned on appeal, setting the stage for a new lawsuit. This time, though, Levin appealed to a Jewish "board of elders" in New York to help resolve things. All parties settled in late 1959, and Otto Frank was compelled to pay $15,000 in damages. Enmities between the two men, though, continued on for years. Such, in brief, is the official story of Meyer Levin.

Now, let's engage in a bit of plausible speculation. Let's say Levin is in post-war Europe (he was), fishing around for book ideas. He publishes his little book on the Buchenwald diaries, but it makes no impact, so he is dissatisfied. He then reaches out to his Jewish network in Europe, looking for someone—a woman, perhaps, or a girl—who died in the war, who has a compelling life story, and who maybe was known as a diarist or writer. By chance, in mid-1945 he hears about the Frank family, the loss of Margot and Anne, and the survival of just one family member, the father Otto. This seems to be the perfect situation.

Then, say, sometime in late 1945, Levin contacts Otto about his idea: to produce a realistic diary 'novel' based on Anne and her life. Otto gets to honor his lost daughter, and make some money along the way, if it sells. He figures it's a long shot, but agrees. By early 1946, Meyer completes a draft of the diary (say, "Typescript I"), and sends it to Otto for review. Otto likes it, but is unsure of its quality, and so he passes it along to friends (Cauvern plus unknown others) for comments. Out of this process comes "Typescript II". Then the story proceeds as above. No one but Otto knows that Levin is the author, but he has strong incentive to keep quiet. As the story takes on a life of its own, he certainly can't bring himself to state the truth; very quickly, there is far too much at stake.

Additionally, someone, of course, has to create an "original" diary. We can imagine Levin working in parallel, asking (or paying) some girl to hand-write a version of his typescript. It would not be hard to create two or three notebooks, and a couple hundred "loose sheets" of entries, within a few months. Levin would then have passed these along to Otto for safe keeping.

All this would provide the plausible context for Otto to appoint Levin as his "literary agent" in America, and it would explain the extraordinary maturity of the text. But we can imagine that disputes over royalties led to the above-mentioned legal squabbles that were never really satisfied. Perhaps there was some behind-the-scenes agreement by which Otto would funnel royalties to Levin, we don't know. Evidently it was sufficient to keep both men from spilling the beans for many years. Otto Frank died in Switzerland in 1980, at age 91, and Levin died in Jerusalem the following year, age 76. The truth likely died with them.

An Assessment

What, then, can we conclude from the above account of the history of this most-famous diary? First, it is remarkably contorted. Many hands had a role in the text, at many different points along the way. The 'original' text may have been revised even by Anne herself, which started a long chain of edits, additions, deletions, "amplifications," and God knows what else. Even if Meyer Levin had no role in its construction, all would have to admit that the tangled history of the text introduces many unknowns into the process. "But we still have the original three books," says the apologist; "the A-version is documented, and so we can always check the different versions against that." Yes, but (a) we are trusting that the published A-version accurately reproduces the three hand-written books (why can't we see scanned copies of all three books?); (b) the A-version is missing for over a year, nearly the entirety of 1943; and (c) we don't know if Anne was being accurate and truthful even in her A-version—in fact, we have much reason to doubt this, as Suzuki will explain in detail.

Second, it is rather remarkable how Otto Frank took every opportunity to market and monetize his dead daughter's writings. Perhaps he was just trying to "honor her memory," as the traditionalists claim, or—perhaps it was a path to fame and fortune. The constant negotiations, book deals, play- and movie-rights, legal squabbles…it all comes across as crude profiteering off a tragic situation. But this, of course, is in keeping with longstanding Jewish tradition: money above all!

Third, by almost any standard, "Anne's diary" counts as a literary fraud. The "diary" is simply not what is portrayed: the daily thoughts and experiences of a 13/14-year-old, trapped in a house during wartime. Given the fact that, among the millions of readers, virtually no one reads the A-version (or even knows of its existence), people are exposed to a highly edited, altered, polished, and "amplified" version, at best. This is no longer the actual diary of an actual girl who lived in Amsterdam.

Fourth, all of this is to say nothing of the many problems, inconsistencies, and absurdities of the text itself and of Anne's alleged 'hideout.' Just to take one ridiculous example, consider that Otto Frank, with the Nazis breathing down his neck, chose as a hiding place for his beloved family…*the backroom of his own office building.* It was a small building, like all old houses in central Amsterdam, and Otto had been working there since 1938 with his local herb and spice business, Pectacon. And yet, given the option to flee to the countryside or at least to some obscure building in the city, Otto chose his own office at 263 Prinsengracht. It's like a bad joke. Faurisson presses this very point:

> When one has a whole year to choose a hiding place, does
> one choose his *office?* Does one bring his family there?
> And a *colleague?* And the colleague's family? Do you

choose a place full of "enemies" where the police and the Germans would come automatically to search for you, if they do not find you at your home? (sec. 10, p. 151).

Then in the following paragraph, Faurisson writes:

> In order to dispute the authenticity of the story, one could call upon arguments of a psychological, literary, or historical nature. I will refrain from that here. I will simply remark that the *physical* absurdities are so serious and numerous that they must have an effect on the psychological, literary, and historical levels. (italics added)

Many of these issues are covered in the text to follow here. In the end, Faurisson offers a scathing indictment:

> Mr. Frank is a story-teller who has given himself away. … The Diary cannot be in any way authentic. … The inconsistencies of the various texts are of all kinds. They concern the language and the style, the length and the form of the pieces that make up the Diary, the number and the kind of anecdotes reported, the description of the premises, the mention of material realities, the dialogues, the ideas exchanged, the tastes expressed; they concern the very personalities of the principal characters, to begin with the personality of Anne Frank, a personality which gives the impression of living in a world of pure fiction. While offering himself as personal guarantor of the authenticity of this work, which is only fiction, Mr. Frank, who has besides obviously intervened at all stages of the genesis of the book, has signed what it is appropriate to call a literary fraud. *The Diary of Anne Frank* is to be placed on the already crowded shelf of false memoirs. (secs. 93-102)

Faurisson stops short, however, of naming anyone other than Otto Frank for the fraud. This seems implausible; Suzuki offers a good argument to the contrary.

Such is the conventional account of the famous diary of Anne Frank. We turn now to Haemer's Introduction, and then to Suzuki's main text.

INTRODUCTION
KARL HAEMERS

The Diary of a Young Girl...or Her Father, or Her Father's Associate the Propagandist

In these times of ubiquitous deceit, explorations of previous unresolved mysteries are inevitable. As people become more aware of the lies, cover-ups, pretenses and marketing stories that attend such affairs as 9/11, weapons of mass destruction in Iraq, the 2009 Swine Flu H1N1 scare, and of course the Covid-19 phenomenon, among many others, we are going to wonder again about the validity of stories long past. If a "mass shooting" depicted in today's media is shown to be some form of hoax, then what about past shootings which we've already accepted? Many people now know the assassination of John F. Kennedy on 22 November 1963 in Dallas Texas is attended by many unanswered questions involving the CIA, the Israeli Mossad, organized crime, Vice President Lyndon "Baines" Johnson, the US Secret Service, the autopsy doctor, and many others. Some of these questions have indeed been answered, and interest continues.

The history of mass deception gathers interest as current mass deception is revealed or at least suspected. This is especially true of past deceptions whose implications still affect us today. An outstanding example is the Diary of Anne Frank, also called The Diary of a Young Girl (does the second title carry more pathos?). Currently, the Anne Frank House is the official curator of the Diary; they serve as promoter and educator on the story, and as custodian of the "annex" house where Anne hid for two years from rapacious implacable "Nazis" in Amsterdam, the Netherlands, and which is now operated as a museum.[1]

Other works have explored the validity of the Diary on numerous points. They raise such questions as: Are the writing style itself and sub-

---

[1] See www.annefrank.org.

ject matters possible for a girl of from thirteen to fifteen years? What are the results of forensic analysis of the paper and ink used, and of handwriting analysis? Numerous editions of the Diary have been published in different languages at different times; are they consistent with each other or do the contents change? The present book is the first of which I am aware to present a graphic display of the various changes. Internal inconsistencies, logical impossibilities and logistical improbabilities in the text have been explored, and more are continually discovered.

This book will present some of the analysis made by perhaps the foremost Diary revisionist, Robert Faurisson (1929-2018). His essay "Is the Anne Frank Diary Genuine?" was considered the first earnest examination of the validity of the Diary, and either the most persuasive or the most notorious, depending on perspective. Faurisson also revised views of the Holocaust in general, for which he was attacked in multiple ways, including physically. Personal slanders, such as "holocaust denier" and "anti-Semite," have been used (and still are used) to try and discredit his work on Diary revision, but this is unjust. Faurisson and all Diary revisionists must be assessed based on the content of their presentation on this topic alone. Personal attacks and references to other works are inadmissible.

Another compelling work examining the validity of the Diary is *Anne Frank's Diary, A Hoax* by Ditlieb Felderer.[2] First published by Bible Researcher in Sweden in 1978 and subsequently in English by the Institute for Historical Review the next year, this work remains an excellent source of analysis. In the Foreword we read "The colossal hoax surrounding the Anne Frank Diary is so immense, the implications so profound, that mankind must find out about it."

"Find out about it" is what we do in this work. An exploration of the various claims for the physical Diary and/or diaries themselves presents the significant confusion over the number of notebooks, their color, size, page count and other logistics of the original physical diaries. As noted in the Foreword, there are three physical diaries; the first is on display, but

---

[2] Ditlieb Felderer, *Anne Frank's Diary: A Hoax,* Institute for Historical Review, 1979 (available on www.archive.org).

the other two are kept locked away on-site. At the time, Otto Frank refused Felderer's request to examine the original Diary itself.

Felderer makes a great contribution through his examination of internal inconsistencies and practical impossibilities within the Diary entries. He explores such topics as the working of the bookshelf door, the noise the occupants made while trying to remain hidden, their gluttonous food supply, various window anomalies, and other suspect accounts. He also identifies perverse and degraded themes, including anal fixation, sexual obsession, genital anatomy, drug use (Anne daily popped valerian pills[3]), and animosity and violence. Though the Diary is marketed as a charming, touching account of an innocent girl facing desperate difficulty while trying to grow up into a young woman, Felderer does well to show us that the Diary content actually depicts a perverted, corrupt, sensationalist account of a girl concerned with debased and degenerate thoughts. Could such thinking occur in a thirteen-year-old girl?

This new book will expand on such themes and add new ones. The Diary contains a great many entries revealing the grotesque and debased direction of the author's thoughts, obvious to those able to extricate themselves from the present-day cult programming that frames the Diary and see it at face value. How such a virtually pornographic work could be so widely promoted for children to read is a mystery only to those who do not realize the perversion of children and youth is, plausibly, one of the objectives of the Diary. Sympathetic identification with the main character is the vector for such filth to spread.

Another critical work emerged in 1998 from Heretical Press, written by British activist Simon Sheppard. *Anne Frank's Novel: The 'Diary' is a Fraud* contains 18 chapters, some of them similar to chapters in Felderer's work. Such topics as "The Manuscripts", "The Matter of the Ballpoint Pen", "The Need for Silence in the Annexe", "Valerian Pills", "The Gassings and Other Mysteries" and others appear to discover similar issues as Felderer and Faurisson. The book is available for sale online but

---

[3] Valerian is an over-the-counter herbal remedy for stress and sleep disorders.

only as an e-book, and shows the Table of Contents and part of the first chapter.[4]

Sheppard has been imprisoned for his "heretical" views, including "anti-Semitism" and inciting racial hatred, in Britain. He and a colleague attempted to escape to the US and apply for political asylum, claiming the law of 1290 expelling Jews from Britain had never been legally rescinded. His request was rejected and Sheppard endured years in prison.

We can see that in the case of Anne Frank's Diary, and the Holocaust in general, freedom of speech can be very expensive. Faurisson was fined, beaten, and fired, Simon was imprisoned, and others such as 90-year-old Ursula Haverbeck and Alfred and Monica Shaeffer have faced persecution, discrimination, assault, prison, impoverishment and ostracism for expressing doubts about the Diary and the Holocaust. Currently 16 European nations and Israel criminalize "Holocaust denial" in various forms, which includes Diary doubt, and others regularly threaten to join them, including the USA and Canada. Iran, by contrast, is particularly noted for freedom of speech on the Holocaust, and awarded Faurisson a prize for his courage in speaking freely.

*****

Perhaps the core of the critique on the Anne Frank Diary focuses on who the actual author was. This takes a surprising wide range. Sheppard in 1996 claimed the Diary was initially written by Anne, but then so distorted by Anne and embellished by another or others as to become a fictional account:

> [T]he Diary is not a forgery, but that the fraudulence it contains is due to a cumulation of distortions started by Anne Frank herself. Indeed it is proposed that it is worse than a

---

[4] Two years prior, in 1996, Sheppard presented a shorter treatise on the Diary, "On the Book of Frank," available online at www.heretical.com.

forgery by being a more convincing hoax: it is an unreliable mixture of fact and fantasy.[5]

Faurisson, who interviewed Otto Frank in person, leans toward the view that the Diary was written by Otto, or at least substantially modified by him. Portions of this book will explore Faurisson's views in more detail.

Felderer presents no conclusion nor even a clear speculation. In a section headed "Did Anne Frank Even Exist?," he writes:

> In fact, it is because the girl existed that the story is so grave, so ugly. The big problem that Mr. Frank has is not that he has no diary, but THAT HE HAS A DIARY OR DIARIES. With every hoax there must be elements of truth or it won't succeed... No serious faker wanting to succeed would (use only fake materials). Instead he tries to get as close to the original as he possibly can.[6] (caps original)

Felderer speculates broadly regarding his handwriting analysis:

> In summing up our observations it seems to us that the handwritings may not at all belong to Anne. The question is to whom; and when it was written? Do they belong to Anne, to Margot, to Dussel, to Mr. or Mrs. Van Daan, to Anneliese Schutz, to Mr. Frank, to his present wife "Fritzi," to Isa or Albert Cauvern or someone else or may they even be a combination of various handwritings from different people?

In an appendix at the back of Felderer's Hoax, he features a quote by Faurisson:

---

5 Sheppard, "On the Book of Frank."
6 Felderer, p. 74

> Unless Anne Frank has risen from the dead to transform
> and alter the text of her Diary, then we must conclude that
> her father has been the author all along.[7]

Felderer includes no speculation in his long list that the Diary was written by Meyer Levin, but this may be because Felderer is examining exclusively the handwriting here. Meyer may have written the content of
the Diary, but someone else may have written out the actual entries, to
give them the appearance of having been written by a young girl. Felderer bypasses the Levin-as-Diary-author theory thus: "[T]he court case
concerning Meyer Levin apparently did not concern the diary but a play
built on the diary."[8]

This book will examine the court case more closely, as well as the
background of Meyer Levin. It will make the strongest argument among
those Revisionists who even consider it, that Levin may have been the
actual Diary author.

These researchers/authors and others—Richard Harwood (Verall),
Arthur Butz, Gilad Atzmon, David Irving, Brian Harring, to name only
some—who have presented doubts and even conclusions regarding the
validity of the Diary have all made contributions toward clarity and ve-
racity of such an influential historical document. We aspire with this
book to add to the evidence and analyses which drive conclusions inevitably toward the view that The Anne Frank Diary is an immense hoax
and fraud.

All the many feelings, perceptions, activities, funding, institutions,
programs, "education" and the overall *Weltanschauung* generated by
belief in this supposed historical document, in the form of a diary, must
be revised. The story of an innocent young Jewish girl and her family
and friends hunted and persecuted by evil "Nazis" as portrayed in the
many iterations of the Diary—into plays, films, other books, articles,
lectures and even museums—must crumble under the increasing weight
of the truth. This book is a heavy block added to the weight of evidence

---

7 Ibid, p. 79
8 Ibid, p. 4

already flattening the flimsy structure of lies known as The Diary of Anne Frank. May truth arise from these new foundation blocks and liberate so many believers from the dangerous illusion, and fortify those who doubt with certainty.

CHAPTER 1
ABSURD ON THE SURFACE

Basic Information about Anne's Diary

For the many readers who, like me before writing this book, have never read Anne's Diary, let me explain some basic knowledge. Anne Frank, the main character of the book, is a Jew of German descent. For undisclosed reasons, the Frank family had to move from Germany to Amsterdam, the capital of the Netherlands.

On the 12th of June 1942 Anne began to keep a diary in a red and white checkered notebook that she received for her thirteenth birthday. About a month later, a Nazi "call-up notice" was sent to her sister Margot, and the Frank family moved to the "hideout". From then on, Anne kept a diary of what happened there, what she did and what she thought. The diary ends 25 months later, on 1 August 1944, just before Anne and the other inhabitants of the "hideout" are arrested.

A total of eight inhabitants lived in the "hideout", of which the following four are members of the Frank family:

1) Anne, the well-known author of The Diary.
2) Margot: Anne's sister. She and Anne died of illness in Bergen-Belsen camp.
3) Otto: Anne's father. He was the only one who survived the war. After the war he published Anne's Diary. In The Diary, he is lavishly praised by Anne.
4) Edith: Anne's mother. In The Diary, she is much criticized by Anne. She died of illness in Auschwitz.

In the "hideout" lived three other people, the van Pels family (in the published version, under the pseudonym "van Daan").

5) Hermann van Pels.

6) Auguste van Pels: thoroughly abused by Anne.
7) Peter van Pels: The son of the van Pels family. He becomes Anne's lover in the second half of The Diary.

In addition to these is an eighth inhabitant.

8) Dussel: A dentist who moved into the hideout halfway through Diary. He often quarrels with Anne. His real name is Pfeffer, but I'll use his pseudonym in this book.

Other characters in The Diary support the inhabitants of the "hideout". These are the people with the Pectacon company, founded by Otto:

Miep: A female employee who appears most often in The Diary.
Bep: A female typist who is said to have retrieved the Diary with Miep after the inhabitants of the "hideout" had been taken away.
Kleiman: A male auditor and accountant.
Kugler: The man in charge of the company.

The only exception to this otherwise clear nomenclature is Anne, which is sometimes written as "Annelies" (her birth-name). When I say 'Anne,' I mean Anne as she is depicted in the text of The Diary or Anne who is supposed to have written The Diary. When I say 'Annelies,' I mean the second daughter of the Frank family, who once existed in the real world. I make this distinction because it is unclear whether the Anne of the Diary and the Annelies Marie Frank of the real world can be regarded as the same person. This is a major theme of this book.

Anne's Diary: Three Contentious Issues

The Anne's Diary controversy is not as simple as it sounds. There are several different levels of problems with the Diary, which are both interrelated and independent of each other. This complex and bizarre puzzle can be somewhat clarified by dividing the issues into three basic categories:

1) Whether the book sold to the public is a faithful reproduction of the original Diary, and whether Otto and others who were involved in the publication were committed to doing so.

2) Whether the contents of the purported Diary are (even given a certain amount of exaggeration and embellishment) an account of what really happened. In other words, is the content of this work qualified to be called a diary?

3) Whether the original Diary text was written by Annelies Marie Frank or not.

These are theoretically three quite separate issues, and each can be tested independently of the other two. It is possible for each to be innocent or guilty independently of the other two. For example, it is possible that 1 is guilty and 2 and 3 are innocent. Even if the Diary is Annelies' work, and the content is factual, Otto and others may have altered the original manuscript significantly in order to publish it.

On the other hand, it could be that, logically, even if 3 is guilty and 2 is innocent, i.e. not Annelies' work, it is also possible that the content itself is basically factual. For example, it would be possible (albeit an almost impossible assumption) if Margot, the older sister, had in fact written the diary from Annelies's point of view.

However, common sense dictates that if 3 is guilty, i.e. the Diary was not written by Annelies, then it must have been written by someone else after the war. It is therefore reasonable to assume that the contents are also mostly fictional, i.e. that 2 is also guilty.

So in general, the Anne's diary controversy is a question presented as follows: Wasn't the author a different person than Anne, and therefore the content must be fiction?

The Translation of "Cat" into "Tarantula"?

The lower the number, the lesser the guilt of these three contentious issues. I will therefore begin by briefly explaining the least guilty allegation, (1) whether the book sold to the public can be said to be a faithful reproduction of the original Diary. This has been examined in great detail by Professor Robert Faurisson, mentioned above. He is generally known as a Holocaust researcher, but his original field of study was literature, and he specialized in the analysis of various literary sources. The analysis of Anne's Diary was rightly part of Faurisson's original research interests. His research report is available in book form under the title *Is the Diary of Anne Frank Genuine?*.[1]

As to point (1), you may be wondering why such a dispute exists in the first place. This is because Anne's Diary, in the form of a handwritten manuscript, already existed before publication. So, one would think that if it was published as is, there would be no such thing as a book that was not faithful to the original. The problem arises when we compare multiple versions published in different languages in different years.

The first published edition of Anne's Diary, a Dutch version, was produced in 1947 by Contact, a publishing house in Amsterdam. This was followed by a German version in 1950, but the content of this version is quite puzzling. The original Diary, supposedly written by Annelies, is partly photographed, but almost all the text is written in Dutch. This is not in dispute. Therefore, according to the official view of Anne's Diary, the Dutch version of 1947 is original.

One would normally expect the German version to be translated from the Dutch original into German. However, after a thorough comparison of the two, Professor Faurisson concludes that at least the German version cannot be considered a translation of the Dutch version (sections 72 to 92 of his book/essay). They both say the same thing in the main. However, the differences between them do not go to the level of an inappropriate interpretation of the translation, but rather to the fact that *the meanings of the words themselves are completely different.*

For example, in the entry dated 14 June 1942 at the beginning of the Diary what was "a little plant" (*en plantje*) in the Dutch version is changed to "a cactus" (*eine Kaktee*) in the German version. Similarly:

12 Mar 43: Dutch version "by candlelight" (*Bij kaarslicht*) → German version "By daylight" (*Bei Tage*).

---

[1] Available in essay form here: http://www.ihr.org/jhr/v03/v03index.html

13 Jan 43: Dutch version "some new clothes and shoes" (*nieuwe kleren en schoenen*) → German version "new clothes and books" (*neue Kleider und Bücher*).

13 May 43: Dutch version "as if bitten by Mouschi [the cat]" (*als door Mouschi gebeten*) → German version "as if stung by a tarantula" (*wie von einer Tarantel gestochen*).

Faurisson lists many other examples of this. Additionally, the German version is on the whole much longer than the Dutch version, and the sentence structure appears almost completely different. Furthermore, the Dutch version and the German version sometimes shift the same sentence from one date to another date. For example, the second-to-last paragraph of the Dutch version 27 Apr 44 has been moved to the last paragraph of the German version 25 Apr 44.

This inadequate translation seemed to be officially resolved in 1955 with the release of another German version by a different publisher. The text of the first German version was dismissed as a "mistake".

Anne's Diary officials would like to claim that this is the end of the matter, but that would be sophistry. How could such an improbable translation of the German text have come about in the first place? Above all, why did Otto, who could read German, tolerate and leave such an inappropriate text for so long? This simple question has never been answered. Therefore, the first allegation (1) is completely guilty. How on earth such a completely different version could have arisen is unclear.

Beginning with the first hand-written manuscript, Anne's Diary has gone through numerous versions. Faurisson (sec. 95) lists the following:

I. The Manuscript of Anne Frank;

II. Copy by Otto Frank, then by Otto Frank and Isa Cauvern (Publisher's editor);

III. New Version of the Copy by Otto Frank and Isa Cauvern;

IV. New-New Version of the Copy by Albert Cauvern;

V. New-New-New Version by Otto Frank;

VI. New-New-New-New Version by Otto Frank and the "Censors"
(Church officials);

VII. Contact (Publishing house) Edition (1947).

It is not at all clear at which of these stages, which parts of the text were
changed. It is therefore an eternal mystery at what stage of the process a
translation such as "cat" being changed to "tarantula" in the German version could have come about. Personally, I suspect that a completely new
German text with roughly the same meaning was written up with reference to the original.

A "Hideout" In Full View?

Most readers around the world read only the final book version—
henceforth referred to as English published version, Japanese published
version, or simply English version and Japanese version. Therefore, they
will assume that the original manuscript of Anne Frank's Diary was
printed in book form without any changes, word for word, and they will
not know about this strange and unusual process of publication. But even
if we limit ourselves to the published version, a careful examination of the
printed information will reveal a myriad of very puzzling descriptions.

Most notably, the "hideout" itself and life there as described:

a) The inhabitants of the safe house had not stepped outside the build-
    ing for 25 months.
b) The existence of the safe house was also unnoticed by the people
    around them.
c) If they were discovered, the residents would be taken away the next
    day.
d) Therefore, the inhabitants were not allowed to make any loud noise.

It is important to note the assumptions here. The location of their
"hideout" is basic information listed in the version sold worldwide:
Prinsengracht 263. This is the building where Otto's company is located.
As stated in 5 Jul 42, Otto said, "we have been taking food, clothes, fur-

niture to other people for more than a year now," and "we shall disappear of our own accord." If he had been looking for a "hideout" for a year, how could he have missed the annex to his own company's building? Shouldn't he have found a house that had nothing to do with the Frank family and used a fake name to live there? Of the inhabitants of the "hideout," Dussel was living in the company of Otto, a stranger, so he could certainly be described as having moved to hide. Why didn't the Frank family do it that way?

Now let us examine the overall structure of this building and the "hideout" floor plan. This is the drawing that appears in all the published versions (Figure 1).

Though this diagram does not depict outright lies, some necessary information is omitted, making it difficult to see the numerous absurdities. For comparison, look at Figure 2, which is an image I found on the Internet and edited myself. In this diagram, the left part of the building is the front house facing the street. This is where the main rooms of the company are located. On the right is the annex. What is considered the "hideout" is not the entire annex, but the second and third floors of the annex and the attic.

On the second-floor landing, there is the all-too-famous bookshelf door (secret door), which is the entrance to the "hideout". Importantly, the ground floor and the first floor of the annex are not part of the "hideout" at all. In other words, "hideout" and annex are not equal. In the Diary, the term "secret annex" is always used, which may mislead the readers. This is why I use the term "hideout".

The ground floor and first floor of the annex can be accessed from the front house at the positions indicated by the arrows (2) and (4) in the diagram. In particular, the President's office (8) on the second floor of the annex is visited by outsiders as stated in the Diary of 1 Apr 43.

The sentence "Why don't you go and lie with one ear pressed against the floor, then you'll be able to hear everything." exists in the English version (1 Apr 43). The Japanese version contains a sentence immediately before this, "The guests would be escorted to the president's office on the first floor," which is not present in all other versions today.

Fig. 1 Bantam Books, p. 17 (edited)

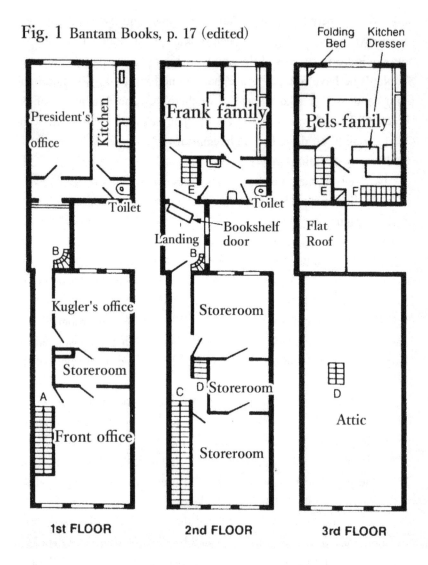

Perhaps this inconvenient part, which existed in the past, has been officially erased from existence. This first floor is really the first floor of the annex, the floor below the "hideout". The Japanese version and the official version of 27 Apr 43 also mention that "The foreign factory delegation is downstairs, and I have to spend my time afraid to even move." This is also cleverly rejected in the English version.

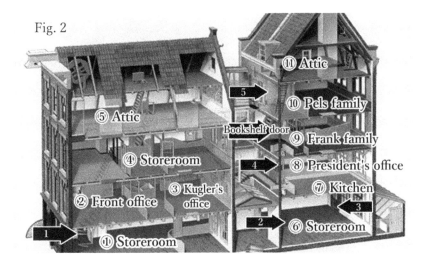

Fig. 2

Moreover, if you look at the structure of the building in detail, you will notice an important fact. *There is not a single toilet in the front house!* Therefore, visitors to the building have no choice but to go to the first floor of the annex to use the toilet. It's almost impossible to remain unaware of the annex's existence. Cleverly, the diagram does not show instructions on the location of the toilet in either version.

Furthermore, this annex is not only accessible from the front house. Figure 3 shows an aerial view of the area around Anne Frank House. Arrow #4 is Anne Frank House. The second floor and above at the back of this building is the "hideout". As you can see, this "hideout" is neither set against a cliff nor surrounded by a deep forest. It is one of a group of buildings built in a rectangle around a courtyard. Naturally, from the courtyard side, the annex where the "hideout" is located is on the front side of the building, and is in full view of the house across the courtyard every day, as shown in Figure 4. You can also enter the first floor of the annex from the courtyard side from the position of the arrow (3) in Figure 2.

Fig. 3   Faurisson Report Photo 2

Fig. 4 Faurisson Report Photo 12

It is an important fact that the space to the right of the landing where the bookshelf door in question is placed (labeled "courtyard" in Figure 5) is shared with the neighboring house Prinsengracht 265. From 265, both the annex itself and the bookshelf door can be seen, as shown by arrows

(1) and (2) in Figure 5. The presence of the annex can also be seen from the landing and the front house as shown in arrows (3) and (4).

Fig. 5

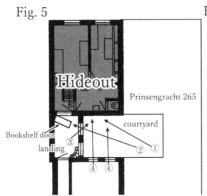

Fig. 6   Faurisson Report, Photo 8 (edited)

Photo taken from inside the landing in Fig. 5.

Figure 6 is a picture of the Secret Bookshelf door taken from directly in front of it. This door can be seen from the neighbor's house from direction (2). You can also see the "hideout" part of the annex from this location in the direction of (3). For some reason, the Diary does not describe any of these very serious facts. In addition, the third floor of the "hideout" can be accessed from the flat roof connecting the front house and the annex from arrow 5 in Figure 2.

On the other hand, in the official explanation of the Anne Frank House, the window in Fig. 5 (4) was "blindfolded with black paper to maintain the quality of the spices". Therefore, the people in the front house were not aware of the presence of the Annex building outside the window. This is too ridiculous an explanation for the following reasons:

· If spices need to be kept away from light, then the room should not even be lit in the first place.

· If so, does that mean that they didn't open the windows in that room even in the middle of summer?

· If they wanted to store spices, they could simply store them in cupboards or boxes that would block out the light. There is no need to darken the whole room.

· As for the window of the landing, there is no reason to blindfold it at all.

As you can see in Fig. 6, the annex is completely visible from the landing. The very existence of the annex itself was not hidden in any way, from the outside or inside of the building. Note that this annex, including the "hideout" floor, existed before the Frank family moved into the "hideout". Therefore, there is no way that the floors above the second floor can function as a "hideout" simply because a bookshelf door has been installed at the entrance to the second floor of the annex.

Even if such a bookshelf door did exist, it could only have the effect of hiding the door itself from the obviously-existing second floor of the annex. However, in the Diary, people who visit the building somehow don't realize that there are floors above the first floor in the annex. This building has been burglarized six times (!) as far as I know.[2] Oddly enough, the thieves, who were supposed to have thoroughly investigated the building before entering, never attempted to break into the annex above the first floor.

In particular, in the famous "Night of Terror" episode (11 Apr 44), the thief is followed by a policeman who comes to the bookshelf door and shakes the bookshelf. However, for some reason, the policeman leaves the lights on from the landing and departs without further investigating the trick of the bookshelf. So the biggest crisis of the "hideout" is over. However, surprisingly, Miep later reported the burglary to the police! (Bantam Books, p. 205). To be honest, the story plot here is beyond comprehension.

We now come to an important fact that makes this "hideout" even more nonsensical. The kitchen in this annex is on the first floor, which is not a hideout. The toilet is barely on the second floor, but it is physically impossible to raise the water to the third floor. Therefore, there is no water on the "hideout" floor above the second floor, and it is impossible to use the water for drinking or cooking. Furthermore, to get to the kitchen from the "hideout" floor, you have to go outside once through the bookshelf door.

Their life here is tremendously absurd. There are eight people living in the "hideout", including boys and girls who are rapidly growing.

---

[2] On 25 Mar 43, 16 Jul 43, 26 Jul 43, 1 Mar 44, 11 Apr 44, and 17 Apr 44.

Therefore, a large amount of food—24 meals a day—needs to be brought in here. These will be brought to the kitchen on the first floor by Miep and other "hideout" collaborators. The four "hideout" women would then have to go back and forth between the "hideout" floor and the kitchen on the first floor, in and out of the bookshelf door on the second floor, to cook it. They carry the food for eight people to the "hideout" floor, and when they are done eating, they return to the kitchen on the first floor, the non-"hideout" floor, to clean up the dishes for the eight people. They ate three meals a day, breakfast, lunch, and dinner, continuously for twenty-five months. In fact, on 8 Jul 44, such an extremely tedious task is depicted in a very humorous way, but in theory it is a scene that is supposed to have continued every day.

Furthermore, the purpose of leaving the "hideout" and going to the first floor is not only for cooking. On 29 Sep 42, it is explained that *everyone* uses the first floor *every day* to bathe.

On 13 Dec 42, Anne boldly takes a bath in the front office of the front house (see Fig. 2), rather than on the first floor of the annex. On 24 Jan 44, Anne and Peter go out of the "hideout" to the warehouse just to see if Boche the cat is male or female. In the first place, according to 21 Aug 42, the bookshelf door was originally created as camouflage for the police who might unexpectedly come in to search. Also, according to the description in the first half of 25 Mar 43, no loud noises should be made inside the building, regardless of the time of day, in order to avoid being noticed by the neighbors, since the building is very susceptible to noise.[3] However, if you read carefully, you will find that the residents are often outside the "hideout" when the business is not open, and they make all the noise they can.

There are other obstacles for eight people to live in hiding. How are they going to dispose of the garbage that is inevitably generated every day? There is no explanation of this in the Diary. The only way to dispose of the garbage is to use the fireplace. However, the fireplace in the

---

[3] "Thin walls" appear in the B-version ("with our thin walls"), the C-version ("with the thin walls"), and in the definitive English edition ("the thin walls"). Recall that there is no A-version for 1943.

"hideout" was first lit on 30 Oct 1942. That is to say, at this point, there were 116 days (!) worth of food waste in the "hideout" during the summer.

Interviewing Otto

Professor Faurisson interviewed Otto in person in early 1977. He asked Otto relentlessly about the physical absurdities of the "hideout" as I have described. Otto was outmatched and finally had to admit that the book-shelf door was completely useless for hiding the existence of the annex. (sec. 41.) He also gave a rather painful explanation that the "enemy" housekeeper would not have cleaned the landings (the presence of the annex would be in full view just by standing there). Then it was conclud-ed that the landings had not been cleaned for 25 months!

Otto's second wife, who was present at this interview, listened to this conversation and finally became angry. She must have realized that her husband's explanation was full of contradictions:

> "Nonsense! No cleaning on that landing! In a factory! But there would have been dust this high!"
> "Nonsense!"
> "What you are saying is unbelievable!"
> "A vacuum cleaner! That is unbelievable! I had never no-ticed it!"
> "That was really foolhardy!"[4]

This is probably the most telling part of the Faurisson report.

---

[4] Secs. 34 and 35.

CHAPTER 2

ABSURDITY LURKING IN THE DEPTHS

Anne's Diary, Revised Critical Edition

Professor Faurisson fought the mystery of the diary using all the materials available at the time. He also thoroughly analyzed the unexplainable differences between the German and Dutch versions. He was able to discover countless logically and physically absurd descriptions in the diary. This alone can only increase our suspicion that something is fishy about Anne's Diary. Undoubtedly, the heart of the matter is the original diary, located at the beginning of the numerous manuscript versions, which was supposedly handwritten by Anne Frank herself. Until we can see it, we only have suspicion.

In the process of planning this book, I got access to the *Revised Critical Edition* (RCE) in Dutch (Fig. 7, 8)—though with a Japanese cover. It is a detailed document, in the original Dutch, of more than 700 pages and contains the most accurate current version of the entire manuscript allegedly written by Anne Frank. This book is virtually unknown to the general reader.[1]

Fig. 7

---

[1] Recall the discussion in the Foreword.

Fig. 8 Example of page

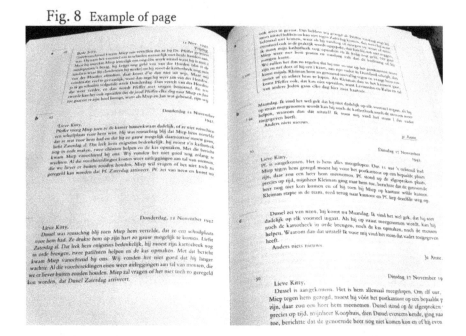

Most readers probably assume that Anne's diary manuscripts are written in chronological order in a series of diary books. However, a diary manuscript is quite a complicated structure.

Here, there are two main types of manuscripts allegedly written by Anne. The first is in the form of a general diary, written in a notebook. As explained in the Foreword, this will be called the A-version (or A-text). Secondly, there is a collection of loose-leaf sheets—between 213 and 336, depending on the source—that are said to be the edited and reconstructed version of the A-version, also written by Anne. This is called the B-version or B-text. It is important to note that the official view claims the A-version was written in real time, in the order of the dates as written, while the B-version was edited by Anne herself after that date.

The A-text was written by hand in three physical books. The first and oldest one, dated 12 June to 5 December 1942, and is a red and white checkered diary book. The second is a notebook with a black cover and dates from 22 December 1943 to 17 April 1944. The third notebook is dated 17 April to 1 August 1944 (the last day) and also has a dark cover.

Notably, there is a large gap in the A-text of over one year: 5 Dec 1942 to 22 Dec 1943.

The dates covered by the B-version are 20 June 1942 to 29 March 1944. As we can see, these two types of manuscripts have existed for different periods of time. In some cases, only one version exists, while in other cases, both versions exist. The following is a concrete list of these, in chronological order:

(1) 20 Jun – 5 Dec 1942:   Both A and B exist.
(2) 6 Dec 1942 – 21 Dec 1943:   Only B exists.
(3) 22 Dec 1943 – 29 Mar 1944:   Both A and B exist.
(4) 30 Mar – 1 Aug 1944:   Only A exists.

Recall Figure 1 in the Foreword for a pictorial version of the timeline.

Did Anne Really Edit Her Own Diary?

First of all, I think many readers may already be surprised at this point. Normally, a diary is a very private thing. It's hard to imagine that she herself would edit the diary she wrote. The official version also answers this question. It is presumably the official view of Anne's Diary, since it is an interpretation by the Netherlands National War Archive, which has done a thorough analysis of the Diary.

Surprisingly, Anne is said to have had hopes of publishing her own diary in the future. The basis for this is some statements in the Diary. Indeed, Anne wrote several times about her dream of becoming a journalist or writer in the future.

5 Apr 44

And now it's all over. I must work, so as not to be a fool to get on, to become a journalist, because that's what I want! I know that I can write, a couple of my stories are good, my descriptions of the "Secret Annex" are humorous, there's a lot in my diary that speaks, but—whether I have real talent remains to be seen. … "Eva's Dream" is my best fairy tale, and the queer thing about it is that I don't know where it comes from. Quite a lot of "Cady's Life" is good too, but, on the whole, it's nothing!

En nu is het helemaal over, ik moet werken om niet dom te blijven, om vooruit te komen, om journaliste te worden, want dat wil ik! Ik weet dat ik kan schrijven, een paar verhaaltjes zijn goed, m'n Achterhuis-beschrijvingen humoristisch, veel uit m'n dagboek spreekt, maar ..... Eva's droom was m'n beste sprookje en het gekke daarbij is, dat ik heus niet weet waar het vandaan komt. Veel uit Cady's leven is ook goed, maar het geheel is niets! (A-text)

And again a few weeks later:

21 Apr 44

I want to send in to some paper or other to see if they will take one of my stories, under a pseudonym, of course. (C-text)

I want to ask [the journal] *The Prince* if they will take one of my fairy tales, of course under a pseudonym, but since my fairy tales have been too long so far, I don't think I have much chance of success. (A-text)

Ik wil bij «de Prins» aanvragen of ze een sprookje van me plaatsen, natuurlijk onder een pseudoniem, maar daar mijn sprookjes tot nu toe nog te lang zijn, denk ik niet dat ik veel kans op slagen heb. (A-text)

And yet again in May:

11 May 44

Now, about something else: you've known for a long time that my greatest wish is to become a journalist someday and later on a famous writer. Whether these leanings to-wards greatness (or insanity?) will ever materialize remains to be seen, but I certainly have the subjects in my mind. In any case, I want to publish a book entitled *Het Achterhuis* after the war. Whether I shall succeed or not, I cannot say, but my diary will be a great help. (C-text)

Nu over iets anders: Je weet allang dat m'n liefste wens is dat ik eenmaal journaliste en later een beroemde schrijfster zal worden. Of ik deze groothand (waanzin!) neigingen ooit tot uitvoering zal kunnen brengen dat zal nog moeten blijken, maar onderwerpen heb ik tot nu toe nog wel. Na de oorlog wilk in ieder geval een boek getiteld «het Achterhuis» uitgeven, of dat lukt blijft ook nog de vraag, maar m'n dagboek zal daarvoor kunnen dienen. (A-text)

The first entry mentioned above is the first entry in Anne's diary in which she describes her dream of becoming a writer. This is at a stage when she has spent over 80% of her 25 months of writing. It is very strange that an adolescent girl who writes a huge amount of text every day and has the writing talent of a professional writer never mentioned this "dream for the future" in her diary until then.

In light of these statements, consider this passage from an entry about a month earlier:

29 Mar 44
Bolkesteyn, an M.P., was speaking on the Dutch News from London, and he said that they ought to make a collec-tion of diaries and letters after the war. Of course, they all made a rush at my diary immediately. Just imagine how in-teresting it would be if I were to publish a romance of the "Secret Annex." The title alone would be enough to make people think it was a detective story. (A-text)

Mr. Bolkestein, the Cabinet Minister, speaking on the Dutch broadcast from London, said that after the war a collection would be made of diaries and letters dealing with the war. Of course, everyone pounced on my diary. Just imagine how interesting it would be if I published a novel about the Secret Annex, from the title alone people would think it was a detective novel." (Definitive version)

Gisterenavond sprak minister Bolkesteyn aan de Oranje-zender erover dat er na de oorlog een inzameling van dagboeken en brieven van deze oorlog zou worden gehouden. Natuurlijk stormden ze allemaal direct op mijn dagboek af. Stel je eens voor hoe interessant het zou zijn als ik een roman van het Achterhuis uit zou geven; aan de titel alleen zouden de mensen denken, dat het een detective-roman was. (A-text)

The official version is constantly appealing to these entries as the reason for Anne's editing of the diary. However, judging from the text of these entries as a whole, that interpretation is highly questionable. Anne was supposed to have written a number of "fairy tales" that she was planning to send to magazines. As a general rule, such a girl who loves reading would probably dream of becoming a popular storyteller in the future. The idea of publishing the diary itself is quite unlikely. In fact, even the entry in question, 29 Mar 44, does not say that the diary itself will be published. She writes that she will publish a "novel of the Secret Annex" (*roman van het Achterhuis*) with a title that could be mistaken for a "detective novel" (*detective-roman*).

The entry for 11 May 44 also says "my diary will be a great help" for a book entitled "Secret Annex" that she wanted to write when the war was over. If it was a publication of the diary itself, the phrase "the diary will be a great help" would not have been used. Obviously, it would be very natural to assume that Anne was writing a novel based on her life in the hideout as described in her diary.

A sentence at the beginning of 20 May 44, which has been hidden from most people's eyes, gives a clear answer to this question:

20 May 44

At long last, after a great deal of reflection, I have started my "Achterhuis," in my head it is as good as finished, although it won't go as quickly as that really, if it ever comes off at all. (A-text)[2]

Eindelijk na heel veel overpeinzingen ben ik dan met m'n «Achterhuis» begonnen, in m'n hoofd is het al zover af als het af kan, maar in werkelijkheid zal het wel heel wat minder gauw gaan, als het wel ooit afkomt. (A-text; see Figure 10)

Fig. 10   Zaterdag 20 Mei 1944.

Lieve Kitty,
Eindelijk na heel veel overpeinzingen ben ik dan met m'n «Achterhuis» begonnen, in m'n hoofd is het al zover af als het af kan, maar in werkelijkheid zal het wel heel wat minder gauw gaan, als het wel ooit afkomt.
| 63   Gisterenavond kwam ik van de zolder naar beneden en | zag[1] dadelijk, toen ik

According to her, the "Secret Annex" was intended to be published "after the war". At that time, however, Anne's life in the hideout was ongoing. She had no idea when the war would end or when such a life would end. If she had intended to edit and publish the diary itself, how could it be "finished in her head"? What would the ending be? Did she even decide on the number of pages? Could Anne predict the future?

Or, was the "Secret Annex" intended to cover only the period prior to this date, 20 May 44?—a rather unlikely assumption. The B-version actually existed until 29 Mar 44. Moreover, there are no drafts of these manuscripts, and very little evidence of revision. In other words, *these are the final manuscripts!* Although Anne says "it will go a lot less

---

[2] This sentence was excluded from the popular "Definitive" version read by most people. It was also not in the B- or C-versions (there was no 'B' entry for that day).

quickly, if it is ever finished.," isn't the "Secret Annex" already finished? Obviously, Anne refers to a "plot of her novel" that runs from the prologue to the ending. That would be the only possible interpretation.

Also, the expression "I started with my Secret Annex" should be interpreted as starting to write the beginning of the novel. If Secret Annex means a publication that edited the diary, why didn't Anne just write "I started editing the diary I've written so far"? Why is the progress of the editing not mentioned in the diary ('A') version, which is supposed to be a pure diary? This sentence should not have appeared in Anne's Diary 20 May 44, but it does. Probably because it was so inconvenient, the published version has this part rejected in all versions as well. It only exists in the official version, i.e. in the A-version. However, the official side unabashedly claims that this statement of 20 May is the basis for Anne's editing of the Diary. I am not convinced at all, but from now on I will accept this claim as a hypothesis and continue my examination.

*****

Let us suppose that it was a kind of camouflage that she wrote as if she had started "writing a novel". I accept the possibility that Anne did in fact start editing her diary at this time. But there's a bomb in this hypothesis that could destroy the very existence of Anne's Diary. Did the people on the official side understand this? I don't think they did.

Recall that official RCE version contains three parallel texts: the A-version original, the edited B-version, and the Dutch published C-version (or C-text). These are published in parallel and chronologically. Texts with the same date appear on the same page wherever possible, and where no text exists for the relevant date, it is left blank. Look again at the example of the official version page shown in Figure 8. In order to analyze this, the key is the period when both the diary version and the edited version existed:

> 20 Jun 42 to 5 Dec 42
> and
> 22 Dec 43 to 29 Mar 44

I have tried to find out what the differences are between the diary ('A') version and the edited ('B') version in these periods. On the back cover of the Japanese edition of Anne's Diary, it says, "the diary written for herself, and the fair copy for publication." When I read this description, I had the preconceived notion that a "fair copy" (or edited version, as I named it) would be nothing more than an elaboration of the diary, with a few deletions, additions, and corrections. However, the reality is not like that at all. In the course of the analysis, it became clear that the true nature of Anne's Diary, which had been hidden from the public eye due to the many layers of information control, was truly astonishing.

Complex and Bizarre! Welcome to the World of "Anne Matrix"!

The first clear date for the diary version is 14 Jun 42. On this date there is only the diary version and nothing for the B-version. Not all entries in the diary version are subject to editing, even in the period covered by the edited version. The entry for this day in the English published version is a greatly shortened version, with some parts written completely differently. The Japanese published version is also merely a greatly shortened version of the diary version.

This editing procedure is, of course, not appropriate from the point of view of faithful reproduction of the original diary. However, it is acceptable for commercial publication. This is because, although the amount of original text by Anne has been *reduced* significantly, it has not been *changed*.

However, the next date, 15 Jun 42, already presents a serious problem. The *first half* of the sentence in the English published version 15 June is taken from the diary version 15 June and the *second half* from the diary version 14 June and combined. Moreover, the text of the Japanese published version 15 June is a combination of the contents of the diary version 15 June and 16 June, with the end taken from 14 June. If there are entries in the diary version and the edited version that have the same date and similar content, it may be acceptable to merge them into a single entry with the same date for publication. However, it is a clear violation of the diary to combine sentences by moving them from the original date to a different entry date. This is because the essence of a diary is that each entry is clearly separated by a date. It is important that there is an unvarnished chronological sequence of specific events that took place on a certain date and the feelings that arose in the writer's mind at exactly the same time. In a diary written by an impressionable adolescent girl, whose emotions fluctuate from day to day, the date is all the more important.

However, it could be said that this violent editing is not yet serious, because it was not done by Anne herself, but by Otto and other editors and translators. *What is surprising is that such editing is allegedly done by the <u>writer</u> of the Diary!*

The next entry in the published version is dated 20 Jun 42, but this entry only exists in the edited ('B') version. In addition, although some of the content of the entry is the same as that of the diary version 15 June and ? June (no date), the text itself is totally different. In other words, this is not an "edited" version of the diary version, but a totally new entry!

Stranger still, there is *another* entry in the edited version with the same date, 20 Jun 42. This is also the case in the published ('C') version. Careful readers may have found this odd, but it is simply the result of following the original. Moreover, this second 20 June is a *totally new text* itself, although it shares some content with the diary version 14 June. The beginning of this entry is as follows:

20 Jun 42
I'll start straight away. It is so peaceful at the moment, Mummy and Daddy are out and Margot has gone to play ping-pong with some friends. (C-text)

Once again, this entry is an edited version. And, as mentioned above, the official interpretation is that it was written just before 20 May 44. This means that Anne, who was nearly 15 years old in 1944, wrote the entry of 1942 as a completely new work, following her memories of almost two years earlier. Of course, the sentence "It is so peaceful at the moment..." could be described as "staged" in a favorable way, but frankly it is a lie.

In the following, I will list the edits during 1942, knowing that they may be somewhat tedious.

- 21 June is an entry that exists entirely in the edited version. There is no corresponding entry in the diary version.
- 24 June is also a new entry only for the edited version.
- 1 July is also a new entry only in the edited version. On the other hand, 30 June exists only in the diary version. And the combination of these two is the Dutch published version 30 June. The Japanese published version 1 July is almost the same text as the diary version 14 June.
- The 5 July entry about the school test results is a new entry that exists only in the edited version. Thus, according to the official, this text was also written in the "hideout" after May 1944. The end of this entry is "Oh, the doorbell rang. Hello [Anne's boyfriend] has come. I'll finish this" (*net belt het, Hello komt, ik slui*) which was rejected in the English version, but is included in the Japanese version. Of course, this is also completely staged. There is no way that Anne's boyfriend showed up at the "hideout".
- The diary version 8 July is a very important entry that explains how the Frank family escaped to the "hideout". The first half of this entry is reflected in the edited version 8 July, and the second half is reflected in the edited version 9 July. The general content is the same, but the text is completely different in each case. In addition, the edited ('B') version includes two completely new entries, 10 and 11 July.

I think it is hard to understand even if it is only written in this way. I've made a diagram—called "Anne Matrix" (see below)—that shows the movement of dates and the relationship between entries.

- The date of the first entry of the diary version after this is 12 July. It seems very strange that there is no mention of the escape in the entry, even though it was written right after they escaped into the "hideout." This was rejected in the English published version of the book, but was retained in the Japanese published version.

- The entry with the date 14 August exists in both the diary version and the edited version, but the content itself, not to mention the text, is completely different. The one used in the published ('C') version is the edited version.

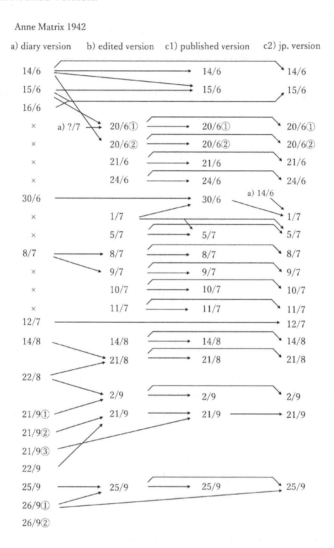

Anne Matrix 1942

a) diary version   b) edited version   c1) published version   c2) jp. version

- Some of the contents of the above diary version 14 August are reflected in the first half of the edited version 21 August, a date that does not exist in the diary version. The second half of the entry reflects that of diary version 22 August.

- The entry with the date 2 September exists only in the edited version. This is a rough combination of the contents of diary ('A') version 22 August and diary version 21 September above.
- There are three (!) entries in the A-version with the date 21 September. Furthermore, although the date of the edited version 21 September is the same, the content is completely different from the diary version 21 September, and the latter part of the content is basically the same as the diary version 22 September.
- The B-version 25 September is a combination of the A-versions 25 September and 26 September.
- In the diary version, we see three (!) entries with the date 27 September. The content of the edited version 27 September is largely the same as the first of those entries. The Japanese published version 27 September is a combination of sentences from the diary version and the edited version. The second part of the diary version 27 September is reflected in the edited version 28 September, which has been published as 28 September in various countries.
- There are three (!) entries in the diary version 28 September. The contents of the first and second entries, and part of the third diary version 27 September are reflected in the edited version 29 September.
- The edited ('B') version 1 October is almost a new work made by extracting some of the contents from the diary version 30 September, 20 October, and 22 October. There is no A-version for this date.
- There is only a diary version in 3 October. The published version is simply a shortened version of the diary version. The Japanese published version 3 October is a combination of the diary version 3 October and 4 October.
- The edited version 9 October is almost a new work made by extracting some of the contents from the diary version 3 October, 20 October, and 22 October. There is no diary version for this date.
- The published version 16 October is composed by extracting a part of the contents from the diary version 28 September, 4 October, 14 October, and 22 October. The Japanese published version 14 October is a combination of the diary version 14 October and the published version 16 October.

Anne Matrix 1942

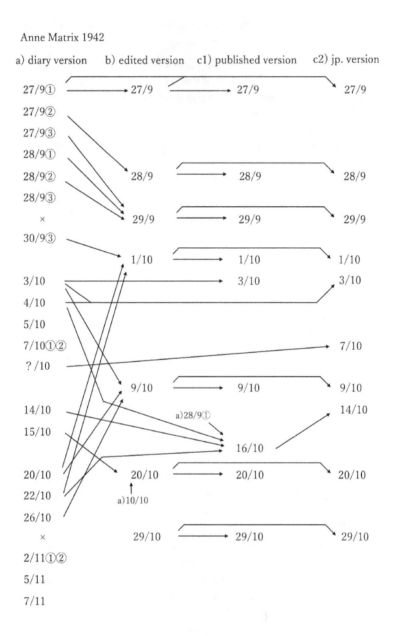

a) diary version   b) edited version   c1) published version   c2) jp. version

- The B-version 20 October is completely different from the A-version 20 October of the same date. It reflects the contents of the diary version 15 October.

Anne Matrix 1942

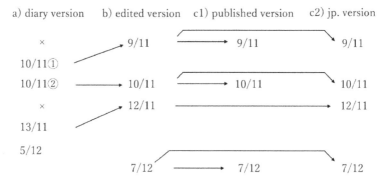

- The edited version 29 October is a completely new entry.
- There are two entries of the same date in the diary version 10 November. A small part of the content of the first entry is reflected in the edited version 9 November, and the second entry is reflected in the edited version 10 November.
- The content of the edited version 12 November is largely the same as the diary version 13 November. The diary version 12 November does not exist.
- The diary version 5 Dec 42 is a very strange entry. It begins, "FOUND LOOSE IN THE OTHER DIARY" (*TUSSEN IN AN-DERE DAGBOEK*) and is written on the last page of the first diary book, just after 13 Nov 42. However, this is an inappropriate position in the timeline. The entries after 14 November should have been written in the (lost) second diary book. The date 5 Dec falls between 28 November and 7 December when applied to the date of the edited version. Why did this entry have to be transcribed all the way in the last page of the first book? The content of the edited version 7 Dec is also related to this, but has serious problems, as discussed below.

*****

At this point, 1942 is over. As mentioned above, after this, we have the period of about a year when only the edited ('B') version exists, so this kind of analysis is not possible. Then, the next three months—22 December 1943 to 29 March 1944—is the period when both the diary version and the edited version exist again.

However, compared to 1942, there are relatively fewer cases of date shifts between the diary version and the edited version. Specifically, for the following dates, both the date and the general content of the diary version and the edited version are, as expected, the same:

1943 →   Dec 22, 24
1944 →   Jan 2, 15, 19, 22, 24, 28, Feb 3

However, in many cases, there are still inexplicable confusions about the date:

- The diary version 6 Jan 44 contains three confessions by Anne. In the published ('C') version, the first two of the three have been moved to the two confessions entry of 5 January, a date that does not exist in the original. The edited version 6 January is a rewrite of the third Confession in a different text, and the published version 6 January is the same.
- In addition, the second half of the diary version 6 January has been moved to the edited version 7 January. The published version 7 January is the same as this one.
- The first half of the diary version 14 February is separated into the published version 13 February. The second half is the edited version and published version of 14 February.
- The edited version of 17 February is largely the same as the diary version of 15 February, with the latter half containing most of the content of the diary version of 23 February.
- The published version 23 February succeeds the edited version 17 February.
- The edited version 12 March reflects the short parts of the diary version 11 March and extends it significantly. The published version 12

March is the same as this. The diary version 12 March is completely different from the edited version 12 March, and the "Japanese published version" uses it as is.

- There are two entries in the diary version 16 March. In the edited version 16 March, there are only the contents corresponding to the second entry, which is said to have been written in the afternoon. In the published version, the date of the edited version 16 March was changed to 15 March, but in the Japanese published version, it is still 16 March.
- The edited version 23 March reflects some of the contents of the diary version 24 March, which is the same as the published version 23 March.

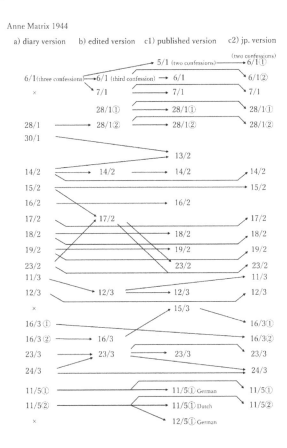

Anne Matrix 1944

a) diary version   b) edited version   c1) published version   c2) jp. version

- In the Japanese version, there are two entries on 11 May, which is the result of a very complicated process. The first is an entry that did not exist in the Dutch version published for the first time in the world, and which first appeared in the German version published in 1950. And in this German version, the date of 11 May in the Dutch version had been moved to 12 May. Later, this original measure in the German version was officially declared to be a "mistake" and both entries were corrected to be 11 May in the diary version.

More Anne Magic!

The long explanation so far has been mainly about changing the date and moving the contents. Personally, I feel that this alone calls into question the qualifications of Anne's Diary as a diary. However, some ardent fans may argue that this level of date confusion is just a small problem. Indeed, if the degree of editing is limited to shifting the date by one day, it may not affect the intrinsic value of the diary. However, what if there are numerous discrepancies between the diary version and the edited version in terms of the facts that happened inside the diary?

First, let's list the discrepancies in individual details:

- A story about bathroom repair in the diary version 28 Sep 42 has been moved to 29 Sep in the B-version. It is about the difficulties the inhabitants of "Hideout" had because of the construction of a water pipe in the bathroom, and the two versions are roughly identical. However, the former says that the work was done on the afternoon of that day (i.e., 28th), while the latter says that it was done last Wednesday (i.e., 23rd), a discrepancy of five days. Why is this?

- In the edited ('B') version of 1 Oct 42, there is a description of the new skirt that Bep bought for Anne that day:

1 Oct 42

Bep bought new skirts for Margot and me at Bijenkorf's. The material is tatty, just like sacking, and they cost 24 florins and 7.75 florins respectively.

Bep heeft in de Bijenkorf nieuwe rokken voor Margot en mij gekocht. Het is rotstof, net jute zakken en kost resp. f 24 en f 7.75.

However, in the diary ('A') version 20 Oct, there is a statement that she got a skirt that is obviously the same:

20 Oct 42

We've now received the skirts. But how ridiculous they are, just listen, mine is miles too long and very tight, and the material is a bit like jute, which they use to make potato sacks. … This kind of thing which the shops would never have dared to sell in the olden days now costs 7.75 florins.

De rokjes hebben we intussen gekregen. Nu moet je eens horen hoe belachelijk, mijne is ellenlang en erg nauw, dan is het soort stof ongeveer als jute, waarvan aardappel-zakken gemaakt worden. [...] Zo'n geval wat de winkels vroeger niet zouden hebben durven verkopen kost nu f 7.75.

In fact, the two dates are 20 days apart. Could the two skirts have been identical? Or were they different, identical in price and appearance? Did they really even exist in the first place?

• The entry of 16 Mar 44 (A-version) contains a short discussion of some meals of Jan Gies, one of the Frank family collaborators. These meals are also described in the 16 Mar B-version, but there are significant differences:

Day	A-version	B-version
11 May	stewed carrots & green peas	---
12 May	stewed carrots & green peas	---
13 May	stewed carrots & green peas	---
14 May	green peas	stewed carrots & green peas
15 May	hashed carrots	stewed carrots & green peas
16 May	---	green peas
17 May	---	hashed carrots

Why is this? Anne allegedly had her original A-version in front of her as she wrote out the B-version; why this discrepancy? It seems so trivial and unimportant—so, why make these changes?

- There is some serious confusion in the episode about Anne's boyfriend, "Hello" (or "Harry"), prior to her move to the "hideout". According to the diary version 30 Jun 42, Anne met Hello outdoors on 29 June, but he left her outside without meeting Anne's parents because he had business to attend to that day. However, according to the edited version 30 June, on the same day, the 29th, Hello is supposed to have visited Anne's house and met her parents! This means that Anne has double-booked Hello in her diary. The published ('C') version eliminates this double-booking by arbitrarily moving the former episode to the 28th and the latter to 2 July.

Also, in the A-version, Anne promised to meet Hello again on 2 July at 8:05, but for some reason in the C-version this promise was changed to 1 July at 7:05.

*****

At this point, some fans might say, "Don't pick on Anne for every little thing!" Certainly, it is possible—though rather unlikely—that these discrepancies were due to Anne's simple misremembering of the date and time, or a careless mistake. But what about the following difference in story? As I have already briefly mentioned, the B-version of 2 Sep 42 contains a close approximation of the first half of the A-version of 21 Sep 42 (despite the 19-day difference in date). However, there are numerous discrepancies between the two stories:

In the A-version 21 September:
- Peter was interested in "a trilogy of books about WW1 with explicit descriptions," but he was forbidden to read them.
- Peter sneaked it out and read it.
- Mrs. Pels didn't know about it yet.
- Mrs. Pels said it was strange that Margot should be allowed to read it; Anne's mother replied that Margot was thoughtful, but that she should still be forbidden to read it.
- Peter was found coming downstairs with the book in question.
- Mr. Pels still insisted that reading should be forbidden, and took the book away.
- Peter was so angry that he hid himself in the attic.
- Mr. Pels took down the folding bed and said that if Peter didn't come down, he would have to sleep in the attic.
- Otto and Mr. Pels put Peter down together.
- The next day Peter went up to the attic again and insisted that he would not come down unless he got the book, but eventually he gave in.

In the B-version 2 September:
- Peter was interested in "a book about women".
- Peter took it to the attic and read it.
- Mrs. Pels was aware of this, but kept quiet about it.
- But Mr. Pels found out and took the book away from Peter.
- Anne's mother said it was all right for Margot to read because things were different between Margot and Peter.
- Peter sneaks the book out and hides in the attic to read it.
- However, when he came downstairs, he ran into Mr. Pels, who slapped him and took the book away again.
- Peter fled to the attic. No mention is made of the folding bed being taken down.

- Mr. Pels shouted "I've had enough of this!" and Otto and Mr. Pels took Peter back downstairs, but Peter finally went up to the attic "again" without apologizing. Peter went back downstairs to bed the next morning. In the evening he went up to the attic again, but was eventually persuaded.

Compare the elements of the two versions of the story. You will see that although the general flow of the story is similar, all the details are very different. There is no way that so many differences could have been caused by misremembering or misunderstanding. Obviously, the editor was familiar with the story of the diary version and used it as a guide *to make deliberate changes*.

And what about the most important event in the entire Diary: the Frank family move into the "hideout"? One would think that Anne's memory of the facts of this period would have been the most vivid, and that therefore she would make no major discrepancies. However, there is an unexplainable difference between the diary version and the edited version in the description of the Frank family's journey to the "hideout" after escaping their previous dwelling. Compare these two entries of 8 Jul 42:

Diary version:
- Anne left for the hideout "by a quarter to eight."
- Anne wore "*two pairs* of pants," a "wool cardigan" (sweater), and a "*hoofddoekje*" (headscarf).

Edited version:
- Anne left for the hideout at "7:30."
- Anne wore "*three pairs* of pants," a "jacket" (*jasje*), a "wooly cap" (*mut*), and a "scarf" (*sjaal*). (RCE, p. 229)

Again, trivial differences—but why any differences at all?

*****

Moreover, it must be pointed out that the discrepancies do not only occur inside the diary. There are also serious discrepancies between the information outside the diary, i.e. in the world outside "hideout," and the diary. The first of these is in the edited version 9 Oct 42:

> The English radio speaks of [Jews] being gassed; perhaps that is the quickest way to die. I feel terribly upset.

In fact, the British BBC first made such a broadcast on 24 June 1942. The reports by a Polish Jewish organization were sent to members of the British Polish Government in exile, which led to its broadcast with the help of the BBC. Three months later, on 27 September,

> the BBC repeated the gassing claim, saying that 16,000 French Jews had been gassed on a train after it had been 'hermetically sealed' and that 11,000 Polish Jews had been put to death in the same way.[3]

The date of the diary, however—9 October—is quite different. Anne seems to have written "I feel terribly upset" in the entry, but this is an edited version; the A-version has no "gassing" at all. Remember that she wrote the B-version after May 1944. It was not written immediately after the broadcast. The Frank family listened to the radio broadcast every day, and Miep visited them every day, so if something shocking like the gassing was broadcast on the radio, it would have been brought to their attention immediately. In fact, the B-version 9 October states "I couldn't tear myself away while Miep told these dreadful stories". Strangely enough, however, there is no such event as the equivalent of "I feel terribly upset" in either 30 June or 28 September, immediately after the above broadcast. The story of the gas execution itself does not exist in the diary version, not only on this date, but on *any* date.

*****

---

[3] Samuel Crowell, *The Gas Chamber of Sherlock Holmes* (2011, p. 17).

There is a more serious problem with the discrepancy in dates in the edited version 27 Feb 43. In this entry, it says that the building where Anne and her friends were hiding had been sold by the owner—without informing Kraler and Koophuis. It also says that the new owners visited the house. The official version states that the sale was a definite fact.

However, the actual date of the sale is 22 Apr 43, two months after the date in the diary, 27 February (see Figure 12).

Fig. 12

* Op 22 april 1943 heeft F.J. Piron het pand Prinsengracht 263 gekocht van M.A. Wessels. (*Het kadaster en de openbare registers in de provincie Noord-Holland*, koopakte 3305 nr. 4).

355

Again, as the entry states that the sale of the building took place without prior notice, the Franks would not have known about it until after the sale was completed. This 27 Feb is the edited version, and the original diary version entry may theoretically have existed. However, unfortunately, this is a period when the diary version does not exist. It would be unnatural for such a serious event not to have been recorded in an entry somewhere in the lost notebook. Alternatively, the date in the diary version may have been immediately after the sale. But then the editor would have shifted the date of the sale by two months when he wrote the edited version. Why?

By the way, the new owner of this building is described as having left without even looking at the "hideout" part of the annex for some reason. Why?

True Emotions?

Even with these facts established, avid fans of Anne's Diary may still argue as follows: "It is true that there may be some minor factual discrepancies and a certain amount of intentional exaggeration and staging. However, this does not detract from the value of the diary in any way. What's important is Anne's *emotions* and *sensibilities* as they are, shining in the midst of despair!"

I admit that there is a certain amount of persuasiveness in this argument. However, this is on the condition that what is written in the diary *is actually Anne's emotions and sensibilities as they really are*. But what if even that is doubtful?

As mentioned above, there are both diary version and edited version in the third period from 22 Dec 43 to 29 Mar 44. There are relatively few edits that are not appropriate for a diary, such as moving dates and sentences around. In many entries, the contents of the diary version and the edited version are similar in the main, and the changes are limited to individual contents and sentence expressions.

However, such changes are far more problematic *as a diary*. In the first half of 22 Dec 43, both the diary version and the edited version describe Anne's illness and its treatment. Although the text in the edited version is completely new, there is no essential difference between them. However, the second half is completely different.

First, the second half of the A-version is quoted below:

> *Ausnahmsweise* (another word is inappropriate here), we are on good terms here, nobody is quarrelling, but it won't last long, we haven't had such a domestic disturbance for at least six months.
>
> Bep is still separated from us, but soon that sister will be germ-free, she was so happy with my Saint Nicholas gift that she brought me an apple, a bag of meringues, Libelle's etc. For Christmas, I also have something for her. For Christmas I also have something for Miep and Bep. I did save up sugar from my dad for a month and I got a pound for St Nicholas, but I didn't take into account that the shops were so busy before St Nicholas. Kleiman has now had the breastplates made for Christmas. For Channukah Margot

and I got a gingerbread and an apron from upstairs, Peter also a gingerbread and 3 meat coupons.

Mr. Pf. gave Mrs. v. P. and mother a beautiful cake as a present. We thought that his wife had baked it, but Miep told father that Mrs. Pfeffer knew nothing about the cake and that she had baked it at Pf.'s request. In addition to all that work, Miep also had to do that.

For St. Nicholas and Christmas, we all received from the distribution 180 grams of oil, 1 ounce of candy and a jar of household syrup. From the candy I treated Kugler, Mr. Pf., Margot, Mrs. and myself. Only the ladies and the children got candy, since we still have 5 cards. Margot and I received a little brooch with a slice and a penny in it; the whole thing shines beautifully, almost all members of the female side of the Secret Annex have such a thing, including Peter. So that's Miep, Bep, Mrs. Kleiman, Margot, Anne and Peter; Mrs. Pf. also has one. That's enough for today, until the next time Kitty, yours, (translated diary version).

In the edited ('B') version, however, this whole series of descriptions is deleted. In its place, there is a complaint about Mr. Pfeffer's acting as a doctor and putting his head on Anne's chest when she has a cold. And the sentence about a "happy Christmas" was replaced with the following short description:

> There is not much news to tell you; Bep is still parted from us, we received extra oil for Christmas, sweets and syrup, the present is a brooch made out of a one-cent piece, and shining beautifully. Anyway lovely but indescribable.
>
> It is drizzly weather, the stove smells, the food lies heavily on everybody's tummy, causing thunderous noises on all sides, the war at a standstill, morale rotten.
>
> *Veel nieuws is er niet te berichten; Bep is nog steeds van ons gescheiden, we krijgen voor Kerstmis extra olie, snoep en*

*stroop, het cadeau was een broche gefabriceerd uit een plak
'cent en dat netjes glimmend. Enfin niet uit te leggen prachtig.*

*Het weer is druilerig, de kachel stinkt, het eten drukt
zwaar op aller magen wat van alle kanten donderende ge-
luiden veroorzaakt, oorlogsstilstand, rotstemming* (edited
version)

You will see that there is a striking difference between the two. The diary
version shows how the people in the "hideout" share a little pre-
Christmas happiness, despite the lack of supplies. It's a life described as
"Exceptionally, we are on good terms here, nobody is quarrelling, but it
won't last long, we haven't had such a domestic disturbance for at least
six months". However, the Editor (Anne?) changed this sequence of
events as "Not much news to report".

In the diary version, the "little brooch made of coins" is a symbol of
the small happiness and solidarity that the "hideout" people have found
in their hard life. However, the edited version doesn't mention that everyone got this same thing.

As a result, the edited version 22 Dec 43 shows Anne's depressing
days as she is still recovering from her illness. In contrast, the second half
of the Japanese version is an original edit of both versions, giving the
impression of being somewhere between the two. Perhaps the translator
felt it would be unnatural to delete all the happy memories.

A similar problem exists in the edited version 7 Dec 42. This entry
is about the St. Nicholas Holiday event on 5 December, and Anne is giv-
en a doll as a gift. The Hanukkah event on 4 December, the day before, is
also mentioned, but described as "we didn't make much fuss". However,
the diary version 5 Dec describes the same Hanukkah event as "the room
was already strewn with flowers" (*daar was het al bezaaid van bloemen*)
and "Last night was wonderful" (*Gisterenavond was het heerlijk*). Anne
and Margot also received a sewing box, a chocolate bar, a silver plate,
and a key to attach to their diary. Obviously, these are better than the gift
of the next day. However, in the edited version 7 Dec, these are simply
written as "a few trifles". Clearly, the happy memories of 4 Dec have
been deleted.

Unfortunately, the second diary book is lost (?), so it is unclear whether the St. Nicholas Holiday event is described in the A-version or not. In any case, if the contents of these two entries were true, it would mean that for two days in a row, a major event and gift exchange had taken place.

Was it true? In the English version, only the edited version is used, so most readers will not notice this unnaturalness.

The Surprising Origins of "Dear Kitty"

At the time this book was planned, I was only interested in one thing: Is Anne's Diary really written by Annelies? However, in the process of analysis, what became clear to me was a "fact" that I had never expected. Even if we exclude the issue of "who the author is," Anne's Diary doesn't qualify as a diary in the first place.

Once again, please check the entire "Anne Matrix". Just by looking at the reality of such reckless editing, this work cannot be described as a Diary in the least. However, if the writing of the B-version was done in parallel with the writing of the A-version, roughly according to the dates given, then the problem may be less severe. However, as mentioned above, according to the official view, the edited version was written in only 80 days, from around 20 May 44 to 4 Aug 44, when she was taken away.

But the defender of Anne says: "No, indeed, she wrote in her diary that she started writing *Secret Annex* in the entry of 20 May 44, which may be read as if she had been editing the diary from that time. However, in reality, she was already planning to publish the diary from June 1942, when she started writing it, and she must have been writing the diary version and the edited version at the same time. That must be it."

However, there is one fact that disproves this. It is a crucial fact about the all-too-famous "Dear Kitty" that most readers of Anne's Diary around the world never knew. The very first diary entry is as follows.

> I hope I shall be able to confide in you completely, as I have never been able to do in anyone before, and I hope

that you will be a great support and comfort to me. Anne
Frank. 12 June 1942 (A-version)

Anne Frank. 12 Juni 1942.
*Ik zal hoop ik aan jou alles kunnen toevertrouwen, zoals ik
het nog aan niemand gekund heb, en ik hoop dat je een
grote steun voor me zult zijn.*

Now, here's a question: Who is "you" in this sentence?

If you have any knowledge of Anne's Diary, you can easily answer
this question. Of course, "you" means "diary book". In fact, in the timeline, the next dated entry, 14 June, is as follows:

I'll start with the moment I got you, or rather saw you lying
on my birthday table, (A-version)

*Ik zal maar beginnen vanaf het ogenblik dat ik je gekregen
heb, dus dat ik je heb zien liggen op mijn verjaardags tafel,*

Now let's ask the next question: What is the "name" that Anne gave to
her diary? Many people will immediately answer, "Kitty". It is so well
known that Anne's Diary begins with the words, "Dear Kitty". But that is
both right and wrong. As a matter of fact, in the early entries of the A-
version, it does *not* start with the words "Dear Kitty". Almost all readers
do not know this fact because they read only the version sold to the public. The following is all the diary version:

Monday 15 June, 1942
I had my party on Sunday afternoon…

Friday, June 19, 1942
This morning I was at home, I slept a long, long time, then
Hanneli came and we had a bit of gossip.

Tuesday, June 30, 1942.
I still have to give an account of the whole week.

Wednesday, July 8, 1942
I still have a whole lot to write in my diary…

Thursday, July X, 1942[4]
I may have already written, but I'm not sure, that we are now in hiding at 263 Prinsengracht…

Friday, Aug. 14, 1942
There is little change in our life here.

22 August 1942
Miep and Jan were at Mr. Goldsmith's…

As you can see, all entries are started *without* the note "Dear Kitty". This policy will continue until this next entry of date.

21 September 1942
I do a lot of work, although I say so myself.

And in the final part of this entry, there is the following text:

I feel like corresponding with someone, and I'll do that with my diary from now on. So now I am writing in letter form which in fact amounts to the same thing.
Dear Jettje, (I will say this,)…

Ik heb zo'n zin om met iemand te corresponderen, en dat zal ik dan in het vervolg maar met mijn dagboek doen. Ik schrijf dus nu in briefvorm wat feitelijk? op hetzelfde neerkomt. Lieve Jettje, (zal ik maar zeggen,)…

---

[4] Anne does not list the day in July.

This is the first call made to a specific personality in the diary version. As you can see, the name was *not* "Kitty".

And the next entry in the diary version is "same day" (*Dezelfde dag*) i.e. 12 Sep.

> I still have time tonight dear Emmy, therefore I will just write you a few lines soon…

> *Ik heb vanavond nog tijd beste Emmy, daarom zal ik jou nog maar gauw een paar regeltjes schrijven…*

The name of the second person was "Emmy". And in this next entry of date:

> Amsterdam 22-9-1942.
> Dear Kitty, Yesterday I wrote to Emmy and Jettje, but I still like to write to you… [see Figure 13]

Fig. 13

a

Amsterdam 22¹-9-1942.
Lieve Kitty,
Gisteren heb ik aan Emmy en Jettje geschreven, maar het fijnste vind ik het toch maar aan jou te schrijven, dat weet je ook wel hé en ik hoop dat het wederzijds is.

At last, the famous name "Kitty" appears. However, the entries that follow begin with a range of names:

> 25-Sept 1942. Dear (*Lieve*) Jacqueline,
> 25-Sept 1942. Dear (*Beste*) Pop,
> 26-Sept 1942. Dear (*Beste*) Marianne,
> 27-Sept 1942. Dear (*Beste*) Conny,
> 27-Sept 1942. Dear (*Beste*) Pien,
> 28-Sept 1942. Dear (*Beste*) Loutje,

Who on earth are these people? As an avid fan of Anne's diary, you may be wondering: Are these the same people who appeared as Anne's friends in the early days of her diary? Let's look at the names of Anne's acquaintances of the same age in the entries dated *before* she moved to the "hideout":

> Hanneli ('Lies') Goslar
> Susanne Ledermann
> Jacqueline van Maarsen
> Ilse Wagner

These are the members of the ping pong club "the little bear, minus 2" to which Anne belongs. These four were Anne's closest friends. In addition, Anne's boyfriends were Hello and Petel.

In the diary version 15 Jun 42, Anne's classmates are introduced. However, the names of the series of mysterious friends that Anne addresses in her diary cannot be found in any of them. With only one exception: Jacqueline van Maarsen. Actually, she is clearly a real person. But, interestingly, in the two entries of 25 Sep 42, Anne says "goodbye" to Jacqueline. The reason seems to be that Anne has to live in the "hideout": "I am writing this letter to bid you farewell…"

And the other names in this entry have already been introduced as Anne's classmates: "How is Ilse doing is she still there."

But the names of other mysterious friends reappear again and again, even after this farewell to Jacqueline. The number of times each name appears during 1942 is as follows:

> Kitty: 8 times   Conny: 6 times
> Pop: 7 times   Emmy: 4 times
> Pien: 7 times   Jettje: 4 times
> Marianne: 6 times   Loutje: 2 times

Who, after all, are these people? Actually, the answer is clearly written in 28 Sep 42 (A-version) and the footnote of the official version:

28 Sept. 1942.

In general, to the whole club,

Dear Kitty,

When I'm scared at night I go to bed with daddy, he's fine with it. One night the shooting lasted so long that I gathered all the blankets together and lay down on the floor in front of his bed like a dog. Bye *Kitty Franken* and friend François; from Anne Frank.

Dear Pop, If there is a thunderstorm or if I can't sleep, I may as well stay with Pim, he likes everything. Best regards Kees ter Heul, hello Pop or Emilie ter Heul-Helmer, from Anne Frank.

Dear Phien, When I have to go to the bathroom at night, I wait until papa also has to go, and then we often meet in the bathroom at night.… (RCE, p. 243; see Figure 14)

Fig. 14

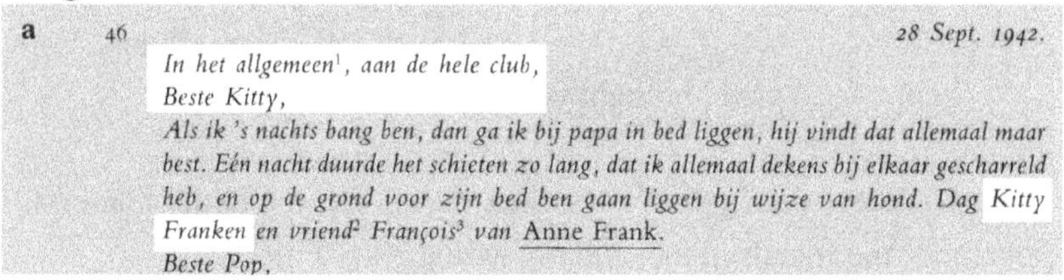

a   46   *28 Sept. 1942.*

In het allgemeen¹, aan de hele club,
Beste Kitty,
Als ik 's nachts bang ben, dan ga ik bij papa in bed liggen, hij vindt dat allemaal maar best. Eén nacht duurde het schieten zo lang, dat ik allemaal dekens bij elkaar gescharreld heb, en op de grond voor zijn bed ben gaan liggen bij wijze van hond. Dag Kitty Franken en vriend² François³ van Anne Frank.
Beste Pop,

The editors of the RCE then include the following footnote:

Mirjam Pressler, the German translator of the present work, has pointed out in the German edition that the names mentioned here by Anne Frank come from a series of Dutch books for young girls named after the heroine, Joop ter Heul.

This is an important piece of information. First, the full names of the people Anne was addressing are revealed here. Secondly, the footnote also explains that these were the names of the characters in the novel. In other words, they are fictional people in Anne's Diary world.

This is probably the reason why Jacqueline, a real person, is distinguished from these imaginary girls. It's no wonder that they are not included at all among the friends and classmates mentioned in the early part of the diary. At the same time, it is clear that the diary itself was also personified in the diary version.

Not only in the early entries, but also in July 1942 (no date), she wrote: "Dear diary, I hope no one ever reads *you* except my sweet adorable husband, and who that is, you know…" This means that at this point in the diary version, the anthropomorphic diary was a separate entity from the fictional girl, Kitty Franken. There is an entry that confirms this conclusively. It is an entry dated 28 Sep 42 but written on the very first day of the diary (12 Jun 42). It is as follows:

> I have had great support from you until now, and also from our dear club which I now write to regularly, I find this way of writing in my diary much nicer and now I can hardly wait for the hour when I have time to write in you.
>
> 28 Sept. 1942. Anne Frank.
>
> I am, oh, so glad I brought you along.

The text clearly distinguishes between "you," i.e. the anthropomorphic diary, and "the friends of the club (including Kitty Franken)".

So how long did this assumption that the diary and Kitty were separate entities last? The clue is in an entry dated Wednesday 22 Dec 43. If you have the English version, check it out. It should start with a sentence like the following: "A bad attack of flu has prevented me from writing to you".

However, this is the result of the edited version text being adopted. The diary version of the same day, which has been rejected, reads as follows:

> Dear Kitty,
> Father has found me a new diary book and that it is of a respectable size, you can convince yourself of that in due course.

> *Lieve Kitty,*
> *Vader heeft toch weer een nieuw dagboek voor me op-*
> *gespoord en dat het een respectabele dikte heeft, daar kan,*
> *je je ten zijnen tijde zelf van overtuigen.*

The "*dagboek*" here does not refer to the "text" of the diary, but to the notebook as an object, which her father found for Anne. This entry is the first one written in the third notebook in the diary version, which is why we have this description. As you can see, Anne is reporting to "you" (i.e. Kitty) that she has got her diary. Then it says, "You will eventually understand" that it is quite thick. This sentence itself is correctly written on the notebook, so if we interpret the notebook itself as Kitty, this sentence becomes puzzling. Obviously, Kitty here is envisioned as a friend in a different place who cannot see and confirm that the notebook is thick.

Furthermore, the cover of this second diary version reads as follows: "Partly letters to Kitty" (*Ten dele brieven aan Kitty*). If "Diary = Kitty," then any text she wrote would be "addressed to Kitty" without exception. Then she wouldn't have written "Partly".

On the other hand, if Kitty is a (fictional) friend of someone in another place, this sentence is understandable. The reason is that not all entries in the diary version start with "Dear Kitty". Only entries which begin with this can be interpreted as assuming that those are letters in the mail sent to a human friend in another place.

Taking all of this together, we have to conclude that "Kitty" at this point in time was a fictional girl named "Kitty Franken," and was a separate entity from the anthropomorphic diary.

Furthermore, the cover of the fourth (i.e. the last) diary version also says this: "Partly letters to Kitty" (*Ten dele brieven aan Kitty*). In other words, even at this point, the Diary was a separate entity from "Kitty". So when and in which version did the anthropomorphic diary change its name to "Kitty"? As for when, as any reader of Anne's Diary knows, it was the beginning of the Diary. In the published version, the third date from the beginning, 20 Jun 42, is written as follows:

Hence, this diary. In order to enhance in my mind's eye the picture of the friend for whom I have waited so long, I don't want to set down a series of bald facts in a diary like most people do, but I want *this diary itself* to be my friend, and I shall call my friend Kitty." (B- and C-versions)

Om nu het idee van de langverbeide vriendin nog te verho-gen in m'n fantasie wil ik niet de feiten zo maar gewoon als ieder ander in dit dagboek plaatsen, maar, wil ik dit dagboek, de vriendin-zelf laten zijn en die vriendin heet Kitty. (edited version)

Needless to say, this is the edited version. After this, the edited version starts with "Dear Kitty" without exception. The same is true for the published version, which is the result of the fact that when both the diary version and the edited version are available on the same date, the edited version was, as a rule, adopted. If you only read the published version, you would feel that the name "Kitty" was given to the Diary in the early days, and that this policy was continued quite naturally. However, when we analyzed it this way, we found that these settings were actually totally changed in the edited version much later. In the diary ('A') version, the Diary and "Kitty" are treated as two different personalities, and there is no evidence that Anne regarded the Diary as "Kitty" until the end.

On the other hand, in the edited version, the Diary is named "Kitty" from the beginning. Therefore, theoretically, the writing of the edited version started after the fourth diary version started, no matter how early it was. (In my opinion, it will be after the diary version is *all* written.)

As mentioned above, the beginning of the entry for 20 May 44 reads as follows: "At long last after a great deal of reflection I have start-ed my *Achterhuis*..." The official position is that this is the basis for Anne's own editing of the diary for the purpose of publication. I have already criticized that interpretation as questionable. However, apart from the issue of the purpose or motive of writing, this is certainly true in terms of the chronological order of when the diary version and the edited version were written. This leads us to the next issue.

All the Diaries Were Written in One Go!

I dare to repeat, just to make the point. As you can see from the Anne Matrix, Anne's Diary has been completely edited, which is inappropriate for a diary. However, if the editing was done in parallel with the writing of the diary version, the problem is still small.

However, it must be interpreted that she started writing the edited version with the setting of "diary = Kitty" only after the writing of the diary version was in its final stages. If we accept the official claim and assume that the editing process started on 20 May 44, then we can conclude that the edited version was written entirely in the last 80 days, until 4 Aug 44 when she was taken away!

However, that would lead to a situation where the truthfulness as a diary of Anne's Diary would be fundamentally disrupted. This is because, in principle, the text of the edited version is given priority in the published version when the edited version exists. There are only a few places where the diary version text is used as is. According to this, the published version, which is known as "a diary of events over a period of 26 months," was actually written all in a short period, mostly 80 days or four months at most.

If so, then Anne, who was fifteen years old, wrote about the entries of 1942 from her memory of what happened two years earlier when she was thirteen. Therefore, these writings do not reflect any of her mental changes and growth over the past two years, nor the growth of her writing ability. When you finish reading Anne's Diary without any preconceptions, you may have sensed Anne's spiritual growth because the early entries were childish and the content became more advanced towards the end. However, it means that *you have been fooled* by the writer's technique. Most of the writings were written at about the same time, so if you feel that the early writings are childish, it is because the writer *intentionally wrote childish writings*.

For example, the early entry, 5 Jul 42, is written as follows:

> Our examination results were announced in the Jewish
> Theater last Friday. I couldn't have hoped for better. My
> report is not at all bad... (B-version)

And the late entry, 7 Mar 44, is written as follows:

> If I think now of my life in 1942, it all feels so unreal. It
> was quite a different Anne Frank who enjoyed that heaven-
> ly existence from the Anne who has grown wise within
> these walls. (A-version)

If you read them without any preconceptions, you would naturally interpret the former as written outside the hideout in 1942 and the latter as
written inside the hideout in 1944. However, surprisingly, the former is
actually written *later* in the timeline! This is because the latter reflects the
text in the diary version as it is, while the former is a completely new
work that exists only in the edited version. Furthermore, "Kitty" in the
former refers to a diary, while "Kitty" in the latter refers to Kitty Frank-
en, a girl in an imaginary world, which is very confusing. Even based on
this alone, such a work does not qualify as a diary. Even with the greatest
concessions, it can theoretically only be a memoir, at best.

However, even so, fans who defend Anne's diary may have the following objections: "If you want to make such criticisms, just read the
diary ('A') version. It's clear what Anne wrote in her diary."

First of all, in response to that objection, I have to point out that, unfortunately, even that is impossible for the period of over one year—6
Dec 42 to 21 Dec 43—where the A-version is missing. And even if that
was miraculously 'found,' we would never know the extent to which it
had been altered or changed.

Of course, if we read only the diary version for the dates that we
have, it might be considered a diary. However, this is on the condition
that the text I call 'diary version' for convenience was really written as a
diary.

Let's read the diary version 26 Sep 42, written to one of the club's
members, Kitty Franken:

> Dear Kitty,
>
> I will only write to you once because I can imagine how you must be feeling right now. Of course it is awful, but Kit I think you will find someone else; of course you think this is heartless, because I know how sincerely you loved Henk and I never expected this from Henk either, but you have a big advantage Kitty, namely you can discuss everything with Mom, I cannot and with Pim I am very confidential but a woman is something else. Let's get rid of it now and not mention it again, because I don't know if you like me to interfere, if you do, you can write me all about him, because you know I will never talk to anyone about it. (A-version)

What do you think? What can we make of this very bizarre text? It seems that Anne is writing about Kitty's love problems. At this date, it has been almost three months since she started her "hideout" life, but she writes as if she has heard about Kitty's love troubles in the past few days. But needless to say, Kitty Franken is an imaginary friend, as Anne admits. She has the same name as a character in the girl's novel *Joop ter Heul*, a personality that was clearly distinct from her real-life friend Jacqueline.

In other words, Anne is writing about the *imaginary* love problems of her *imaginary* friend, and the entire text is a meaningless figment of her imagination. She writes as if she is in correspondence with her, but that is also a fantasy. This is perhaps one of the most inconvenient statements in the many diary entries. This text has been rejected in both the B- and C-versions, and rightly so. If this entry had been published, readers would have been perplexed by the sudden revelation that Kitty, the diary, had a boyfriend!

Similarly, although shorter, there is a complete fantasy in the diary version of the next day, 27 Sep 42:

> Dearest Conny,
>
> How are you and Nanny, poor soul you are so lonely, yes but here's a fine prospect, you can stay with me, I was with your mother the whole morning, and she agrees, I hope this

diversion is to your liking, come as quickly as possible. (A-version)

Needless to say, of course, Conny's mother is also an imaginary personality. These are, in essence, plays she wrote for her imaginary friends. However, I am not criticizing this kind of writing in any way. Even if I adopt as a working hypothesis the claim that Diary was written by Annelies, I am merely pointing to it as evidence of the presence of pure fantasy in the text.

With that in mind, I want you to read the following early entries without any preconceptions. The text is quite long, but I dare to quote the entire text from the English C-version:

Sunday, 21 June, 1942 Dear Kitty,

Our whole class B, is trembling, the reason is that the teachers' meeting is to be held soon. There is much speculation as to who will move up and who will stay put. Miep de Jong and I are highly amused at Wim and Jacques, the two boys behind us. They won't have a florin left for the holidays, it will all be gone on betting. "You'll move up," "Shan't," "Shall," from morning till night. Even Miep pleads for silence and my angry outbursts don't calm them.

According to me, a quarter of the class should stay where they are; there are some absolute cuckoos, but teachers are the greatest freaks on earth, so perhaps they will be freakish in the right way for once.

I'm not afraid about my girl friends and myself, we'll squeeze through somehow, though I'm not too certain about my math. Still we can but wait patiently. Till then, we cheer each other along.

I get along quite well with all my teachers, nine in all, seven masters and two mistresses. Mr. Keptor, the old math master, was very annoyed with me for a long time because I chatter so much. So I had to write a composition with "A Chatterbox" as the subject. A chatterbox! Whatever could one write? However, deciding I would puzzle that out later, I wrote it in my notebook, and tried to keep quiet.

That evening, when I'd finished my other homework, my eyes fell on the title in my notebook. I pondered, while chewing the end of my fountain pen, that anyone can scribble some nonsense in large letters with the words well spaced but the difficulty was to prove beyond doubt the necessity of talking. I thought and thought and then, suddenly having an idea, filled my three allotted sides and felt completely satisfied. My arguments were that talking is a feminine characteristic and that I would do my best to keep it under control, but I should never be cured, for my mother talked as much as I, probably more, and what can one do about inherited qualities?

Mr. Keptor had to laugh at my arguments, but when I continued to hold forth in the next lesson, another composition followed. This time it was "Incurable Chatterbox," I handed this in and Keptor made no complaints for two whole lessons. But in the third lesson it was too much for him again. "Anne, as punishment for talking, will do a composition entitled 'Quack, quack, quack, says Mrs. Natterbeak'." Shouts of laughter from the class. I had to laugh too, although I felt that my inventiveness on this subject was exhausted. I had to think of something else, something entirely original. I was in luck, as my friend Sanne writes good poetry and offered to help by doing the whole composition in verse. I jumped for joy. Keptor wanted to make a fool of me with this absurd theme, I would get my own back and make him the laughingstock of the whole class. The poem was finished and was perfect. It was about a mother duck and a father swan who had three baby ducklings. The baby ducklings were bitten to death by Father because they chattered too much. Luckily Keptor saw the joke, he read the poem out loud to the class, with comments, and also to various other classes.

Since then I am allowed to talk, never get extra work, in fact Keptor always jokes about it.

Yours, Anne

Wednesday, 24 June, 1942 Dear Kitty,
It is boiling hot, we are all positively melting, and in this heat I have to walk everywhere. Now I can fully appreciate how nice a tram is; but that is a forbidden luxury for Jews-shank's mare is good enough for us. I had to visit the dentist in the Jan Luykenstraat in the lunch hour yesterday. It is a long way from our school in the Stadstimmertuinen; I nearly fell asleep in school that afternoon. Luckily, the dentist's assistant was very kind and gave me a drink-she's a good sort.

We are allowed on the ferry and that is about all. There is a little boat from the Josef Israelskade, the man there took us at once when we asked him. It is not the Dutch people's fault that we are having such a miserable time.

I do wish I didn't have to go to school, as my bicycle was stolen in the Easter holidays and Daddy has given Mummy's to a Christian family for safekeeping. But thank goodness, the holidays are nearly here, one more week and the agony is over. Something amusing happened yesterday, I was passing the bicycle sheds when someone called out to me. I looked around and there was the nice-looking boy I met on the previous evening, at my girl friend Eva's home. He came shyly towards me and introduced himself as Harry Goldberg. I was rather surprised and wondered what he wanted, but I didn't have to wait long. He asked if I would allow him to accompany me to school. "As you're going my way in any case, I will," I replied and so we went together. Harry is sixteen and can tell all kinds of amusing stories. He was waiting for me again this morning and I expect he will from now on.

Yours, Anne

Friday, 3 July, 1942 Dear Kitty,

Harry visited us yesterday to meet my parents. I had bought a cream cake, sweets, tea, and fancy biscuits, quite a spread, but neither Harry nor I felt like sitting stiffly side by side indefinitely, so we went for a walk, and it was already ten past eight when he brought me home. Daddy was very cross, and thought it was very wrong of me because it is dangerous for Jews to be out after eight o'clock, and I had to promise to be in ten to eight in future.

Tomorrow I've been invited to his house. My girl friend Jopie teases me the whole time about Harry. I'm honestly not in love, oh, no, I can surely have boy friends—no one thinks anything of that-but one boy friend, or beau, as Mother calls him, seems to be quite different. …

The entry for these dates exists only in the edited version. Moreover, even contents similar to these does not exist in the A-version at all; this text is entirely new. Therefore, Anne had to write all these detailed events, in mid-1944, from her memory of two years ago!

If we are not to accept the claim that Anne has an extraordinary, almost photographic memory, we should at least interpret the dates as having been given in a totally lax manner. And the details of the events must be subject to much speculation or even creation.

In this case, the following serious proposition arises for the whole Diary: *Is there any guarantee that the entries, including all diary versions of the entire period, are the events that actually happened?* In fact, how can we be sure that the date on the diary version means that the text was actually written on that day? *How can we exclude the possibility that all the writing in the Diary was imaginary?*

In fact, this is the most reasonable interpretation if we converge the many lines of evidence I have presented. Consider once again the issue of the date changes. By checking the Anne Matrix, you can see that, for example, the diary version 15 Oct 42 has been moved to the edited version 20 Oct 42, that is, from a single entry to a single entry. Moreover, the contents of these two entries are largely the same. What was the purpose of this date shift? Why couldn't the date of this entry have remained at the 15th? The simplest answer is that the date didn't mean anything important to the writer. There was no particular reason for this date shift. Only by this interpretation we can understand the reason for the exhaustive date merging, moving, deleting, and adding throughout the edited version. In other words, the person who created the edited version *did not consider it as a diary*. If this is to be criticized as an overstatement, then the author was at least willing to let the edited version lose its authenticity as a diary.

Furthermore, the following suspicions inevitably arise:

- The possibility that *all* the characters are in some sense fictional personalities (even if based on a real people).
- The possibility that *all* the stories they acted out, and all the dialogues that accompanied them, were the product of imagination, regardless of which version.
- The possibility that this work is *not even qualified to call itself a memoire, let alone a diary*.

Most of the inconvenient entries in Anne's Diary belong to the diary version, but there is one exception, which belongs to the B-version. It is the entry of 7 Aug 43:

> A few weeks ago I started to write a story, something completely made up, and that gave me such pleasure that my pen-children are now piling up. Because I promised you that I would give you a faithful and unadorned account of all my experiences, I'll let you judge whether small children may perhaps take pleasure in my tales. (RCE, p. 407)

This was rejected in the English version, but is included in the Japanese version, which claims to be the complete version. Interestingly, however, the sentence "Because I promised you that I would give you a faithful and unadorned account of all my experiences" has been deleted. Why was such a step was taken in the complete version which was intended to publish Anne's true story? If you have read the previous analyses, it is easy to understand why. The translator, who knew all the texts, knew better than anyone else that this statement is inaccurate, or to put it bluntly, a falsehood. And she probably felt guilty about publishing this text.

I have already provided more than enough evidence of this. Let's recall once again the example of 8 Jul 42:

Diary version:
- Anne left for the hideout "by a quarter to eight."
- Anne wore "*two pairs* of pants," a "wool cardigan" (sweater), and a "*hoofddoekje*" (headscarf).

Edited version:
- Anne left for the hideout at "7:30."
- Anne wore "*three pairs* of pants," a "jacket" (*jasje*), a "wooly cap" (*mut*), and a "scarf" (*sjaal*). (RCE, p. 229)

Obviously, at least one of these two descriptions is false. Therefore, it is logically established that "Because I promised you that I would give you a faithful and unadorned account of all my experiences" is false. Even more: Can we rule out the possibility that *both* of these statements are false? No, we cannot.

Was Everything a Figment?

In response to this, one might still have the following objection:

> "No, it's just the result of an acceptable arrangement in editing for publication. Also, fantasies about imaginary friends are clearly distinguishable from other real-life events. Therefore, even if there are some girlish exaggerations, fantasies, and slight misremembering, there is no doubt that the descriptions in the diary version are in the main real."

However, even if we limit ourselves to the diary version, which is ostensibly supposed to be a pure diary, there are serious falsehoods. One of them is 21 Apr 44, which I have already mentioned:

> I want to ask *The Prince* [journal] if they will take one of
> my fairy tales, of course under a pseudonym, but since my
> fairy tales have been too long so far, I don't think I have
> much chance of success. (A-version)

This is obviously not true, according to Anne's diary official. This is because the Fairy Tales by Anne, also unquestionably attributed to her, are nearly all rather very short. These tales are published in the RCE edition; it includes 41 separate short stories, nearly all of which are around one page in length. The longest tale, "Blurry the Explorer," runs only about eight pages. What Anne wanted was for her fairy tales to be published in a magazine, but this was probably done to avoid conflicts with the interpretation that she was trying to publish the diary itself.

There is also a serious inconsistency in the unfinished (?) story *Cady's Life* (original title *Cady's leven*), which is also supposed to be Annelies' work. In Anne's Diary, it is only mentioned as a work in progress. However, in the diary version 11 May 44, there is a story plan that Anne is going to write up to the end. It is roughly as follows:

- Cady was a young girl recuperating in a sanatorium.
- There she met a boy named Hans.
- She was later released from the sanatorium and continued her correspondence with Hans.
- She learned of his political ideology in 1941 and became estranged from Hans after that.
- However, amidst various events, their relationship continued.
- Eventually, Cady married another man, but Hans' presence remained in her heart for a long time. (RCE p. 669)

Overall, it seems to be a sentimental adult love story about the relationship between Cady and Hans. Very cleverly, in the B-version, this whole story plan is deleted. (The Japanese version contains the whole thing, in all seriousness.) This is because the story plan Anne describes in her Diary does not quite match the actual content of *Cady's Life* that we can actually read. In fact, the main character is a young girl named Cady, and the story begins with her recuperating in a sanatorium. And Hans also appears in the story. However, out of the 30 pages, he appears in only about 7 pages in the middle of the story. After that, Hans' name does not appear again at all, and the story shifts to her interactions with the woman she met at the sanatorium. Oddly enough, the story has progressed to 1942 and ends with Cady's friend Marie being taken away by the Nazis. Somehow, the aforementioned episode—that she learned of his political ideology in 1941—is not mentioned at all.

The actual *Cady's Life* is, on the whole, more of an allegorical work with an ambiguous impression than a realistic human drama. I can't imagine how the story that Anne describes in the diary version could develop after that. It is also odd because *Cady's Life* is supposed to be unfinished, but as far as the work is concerned, it ends in a place that, while incoherent, seems to be complete.

In fact, however, even this is only a minor issue. What is more serious is the place where this *Cady's Life* was written down. It is the fourth (i.e., last) diary version in the timeline. This notebook is mentioned at the beginning of 18 Apr 44 as follows:

> Someone's been a real darling again and has torn up a chemistry exercise book for me to make a new diary, this time the someone was Margot. (A-version)

Now, compare this to a book by Ernst Schnabel, *A Portrait in Courage* (1958). Page 188 is reproduced below in Figure 16:

Fig. 16

> Concerning the beginning of this novel, Anne had written:
>
> *I have many ideas, and am busy assembling them. But since I have no paper, I shall have to start writing from the back.*
>
> And she took her account-book diary, the one she was currently using, which was to be her last, turned it around, and began *Cady's Life* in the same notebook. Thus diary and novel ran toward one another in the notebook. Some day they would meet, collide somewhere in the middle of the book.

Then, logically, the timeline would be as follows:

1) Margot makes the notebook for Anne so that she can write in her diary.

2) Anne starts writing her diary from the first page of the notebook, from 18 Apr 44.

3) From the last page of the notebook, Anne starts to write *Cady's Life* with the notebook upside down.

However, there is a very strange fact that directly contradicts this. In the entry of 17 Feb 44, two months earlier than this, that is, *from the time when she was using the* previous *diarybook, Anne was already writing* Cady's Life *in her diarybook!* Furthermore, even on 17 Feb 44, "The Life of Cady" is clearly stated to be a work in progress, "not written for a long time":

> I thought I could take my chances now, got out my diarybook and let him read that bit between Cady and Hans about God. I can't say at all what an impression that made on him, ... (A-version; not in B- or C-versions)

> *Ik dacht dat ik nu m'n kans wel kon wagen, haalde m'n dagboek en liet hem dat stuk tussen Cady en Hans over God lezen. Ik kan helemaal niet zeggen wat dat voor een indruk op hem heeft gemaakt, ...* (A-version; see Fig 17)

Indeed, the discussion between Cady and Hans about God exists in "Cady's Life". However, at this point, the diary in which this work is written, the notebook that Margot made for Anne, must not yet have existed in any form. At the time of this entry (17 Feb), the third notebook had been used only up to p. 63. Therefore, if "Cady's Life" is to be written from the last page of the notebook, it must be exactly this third notebook. However, according to the official data, the third notebook has diary entries up to p. 200. Considering the volume of a typical notebook, this may mean that all the pages were devoted solely to the diary. On the other hand, in the fourth notebook, the diary is finished by p. 128, so the number of pages consumed is far less. As Schnabel describes, it is actually the fourth notebook that can afford to write "Cady's Life".

Fig. 17

a 63   Donderdag 17 Februari
                                                           1944.

Beste Kitty,
Vanochtend was ik boven en ik had mevrouw beloofd eens wat verhaaltjes voor te lezen. Ik begon met Eva's droom, dat vond ze erg leuk, toen las ik nog een paar dingen uit het Achterhuis waar ze om schaterden. Peter luisterde ook gedeeltelijk (ik bedoel alleen bij het laatste) en vroeg of ik eens bij hem kwam om nog meer voor te lezen. Ik dacht dat ik nu m'n kans wel kon wagen, 'haalde m'n dagboek en liet hem dat stuk tussen Cady en Hans over God lezen. Ik kan helemaal niet zeggen wat dat voor een indruk op hem heeft gemaakt, hij zei iets wat ik niet meer weet, niet of het goed is, maar iets over de gedachte zelf. Ik vertelde hem dat ik alleen maar wilde laten zien dat ik niet alleen maar grappige dingen opschreef. Hij knikte met z'n hoofd[2] en ik ging de kamer uit. Zien of ik er nog wat van hoor!

                                                          je
                                              Anne Frank.

If "Cady's Life" is "written from the end of the fourth diary," then the statement of 17 Feb is logically confirmed as false. And it is clearly beyond the limits of what can be interpreted as a misunderstanding by Anne. And since this is a diary ('A') version, it cannot be interpreted as a deliberate staging for publicity.

*****

In any case, a person who has made so many factual changes and written so many falsehoods is telling the blatant lie that "I promised you that I would give you a faithful report." So what part of the Diary written by such a person can we believe to be a faithful account of real events?

- Why is the physical setting of "hideout" absurd?
- Why are there inconsistencies in the description of sound in "hideout"?
- Why were so many changes made in the edited version that the original form was not retained?
- Why are there not only changes but also completely new entries?
- Why is there an unexplainable discrepancy in the facts between the diary version and the edited version?
- Why do the dates in the Diary not match the dates of real-world events, such as the BBC radio broadcast and the sale of the building?
- Why did she(?) do this kind of editing herself?
- Why are there outright falsehoods even about the work she is supposed to have written?

The answer is obvious: *Anne's Diary is not a diary*, not only in the edited version but in the diary version as well. The person who wrote it was well aware of that.

As many people are aware, there is something called a 'mockumentary,' which is a fake documentary, designed to look like the real thing. In the same way, Anne's Diary is a complete fiction in the form of a diary, and the events depicted, the dialogues of the characters, and even the emotions and characterization of Anne Frank, the supposed author, are virtual. It is no wonder, then, that she (?) had no hesitation in writing the edited version, no matter how she changed, deleted, or moved the diary version, or included falsehoods in the text.

At the same time, Otto and others involved in the publication of the published version were well aware of this. I have already mentioned that the first German version published was almost a different text from the Dutch version, with shifting dates and descriptions, and could not be called a translation in the least. If Otto had an attachment to the original text as being the legacy of his late daughter's writing, it is extremely strange that he would have allowed such a German version to be published.

In other words, Otto, like the authors of the edited version, was not particular about whether the date and content had to be faithful to the original. They thought that as long as the content roughly matched, there wouldn't be a problem. By interpreting it in that way, this question is cleared up.

This conclusion of mine is logically independent of the question of who is the author of Anne's Diary. *Even if* Annelies was the author as the official version claims, it does not change the fact that this work has *no truthfulness as a diary at all*. In light of this, I conclude that a girl named Annelies Marie Frank could *never* have been the author of the A-version or the edited B-version.

CHAPTER 3
ANNIE AMPLE: A SOFT-CORE PORN ROMANTIC LIFE?

This is only the beginning, however. One finds very serious confusions and shocking statements in the 1944 entries, regarding Anne's romantic feelings and sexuality. The first of these can be seen as early as 6 Jan 44. Obviously, the highlight of the diary is the love affair between Anne and Peter, and this date is an important entry in the story. Both the diary version and the edited version have the same beginning, as follows:

> My longing to talk to someone became so great that somehow I wanted to talk to Peter.

> *Mijn verlangen om eens met iemand te praten, werd zo groot, dat ik op de één of andere manier met Peter wilde praten.* (diary version)

> *Mijn verlangen om eens met iemand te praten werd zo groot dat ik het op de een of andere manier in m'n hoofd kreeg, Peter daarvoor uit te kiezen.* (edited version)

Anne then ascends to the third floor and faces Peter, who is solving a crossword puzzle. She wants to have a romantic conversation, but Peter, who is shy, is confused by Anne's arrival and doesn't know what to say, so the atmosphere doesn't end up being very lively. And here's how the edited version describes Anne after she went to bed that night:

> At night in bed I found the whole situation far from encouraging and the idea of having to beg for Peter's favors just repulsive. (B-version)

> *'s Avonds in bed vond ik de hele situatie lang niet op-*
> *wekkend en het idee dat ik om Peters gunsten moet smeken*
> *gewoon afstotend.* (edited version)

Anne is very calm. She even hates her own act of trying to get her favor from Peter. However, in the A-version, the same scene was written as follows:

> At night in bed I had to cry, cry terribly and yet no one was allowed to hear. In bed I thought about what I would say to Peter today and couldn't stop sobbing. I fell asleep very late. (translated diary version)

> *'s Avonds in bed vond ik de hele situatie lang niet op-*
> *wekkend en het idee dat ik om Peters gunsten moet smeken*
> *gewoon afstotend.* (diary version)

Anne was so sentimental that she cried until late at night. I get the impression that a love for Peter had already been born in her heart. Moreover, in the diary version, Anne's sentimentality was still strong in the entry of 12 Jan, six days later:

> Last night this suddenly came to me and I don't know what it is, but I can never find the right moment to talk to him. And then...... I cry so easily at something like that and then I can't say everything as calmly anyway, as I want to. (A-version)

> *Gisterenavond kwam dat opeens bij me op en ik weet niet*
> *wat het is, maar ik kan nooit het geschikte moment vinden*
> *om met hem te praten. En dan...... ik huil zo gauw bij zoiets*
> *en dan kan ik alles toch niet zo rustig zeggen, als ik wel wil.*
> (diary version)

In the edited version and published version, these descriptions are completely rejected. Therefore, almost no one in the world knows about Anne, the crybaby.

In the diary version 6 Jan, this episode is the third of three confessions by Anne and is written as "one is closest to my heart" (*en die ligt me het naast aan het hart*). However, in the edited version, this event is not described as being particularly significant. Clearly, the rating of the importance of the conversation with Peter has been convincingly lowered. Incidentally, in the published version, the three confessions are reduced to two confessions, and this event is no longer treated as a confession.

After this, in the diary version, Anne's feelings for Peter grow like a big bang. However, when there are entries with the same date in the edited version, they have all been deleted or modified. The entry for 12 Feb 44 is written as follows, which is common to both the diary version and the edited version:

> The sun is shining, the sky is deep blue there is a lovely wind blowing and I am so—so longing—for everything ..... (translated diary version)

> *De zon schijnt, de hemel is diep-blauw er waait een heerlijke wind en ik verlang zo – verlang zo – naar alles .....* – (diary version)

However, at the end of the entry, the two sentences are completely different. In the diary version, it reads as follows:

> I believe I feel the spring in me, I feel the spring awakening, I feel it in my whole body and in my soul. I have to restrain myself, over and over again, I long for my Petel, I long for every boy, including *Peter*—here. I would like to shout at him, "Oh say something to me, don't always keep just that smile, touch me, that I might get that blissful feeling inside me again, like I first had it in my dream of Petel's cheek!"

I am all confused, I do not know what to read, what to write, what to do, I only know that I longing.
(translated A-version; recall that 'Petel' is the name of a boy Anne was once in love with, before the hideout.)

Ik geloof dat ik het voorjaar in me voel, ik voel het lente-ontwaken, ik voel het in m'n hele lichaam en in m'n ziel.

Ik moet me in bedwang houden, steeds maar weer, ik verlang naar m'n Petel, ik verlang naar elke jongen, ook naar Peter – hier. Ik zou wel tegen hem willen schreeuwen: „O zeg wat tegen me, houd niet altijd alleen die glimlach, raak me aan, dat ik weer dat zaligmakende gevoel in me krijg, zoals ik het voor't eerst gehad heb in m'n droom van Petels' wang!"

Ik ben helemaal in de war, ik weet niet wat te lezen, wat te schrijven, wat te doen, ik weet alleen dat ik verlang.
(diary version)

This description has been changed as follows in the relevant part of the edited version.

I believe that it's spring within me, I feel that spring is awakening, I feel it in my whole body and soul. It is an effort to behave normally, I feel utterly confused, don't know what to read, what to write, what to do, I only know that I am longing… (B-version)

Ik geloof dat ik het voorjaar in me voel, ik voel het lente-ontwaken, ik voel het in m'n hele lichaam en in m'n ziel. Ik moet me in bedwang houden om gewoon te doen, ik ben totaal in de war, weet niet wat te lezen, wat te schrijven, wat te doen, weet alleen dat ik verlang.... (edited version)

In particular, it should be noted that the statement "she is longing for all boys, *including Peter*" has been deleted.

The next entry of interest is 23 Feb 44. The last sentence of the diary version reads as follows:

> And I believe that nature sets all fear at rest for every trouble, even when there are bombs or gunfire.
>
> Oh, who knows, perhaps it won't be long before I can share this overwhelming feeling of bliss with *Peter*. (A-version)

On the other hand, the edited B-version concludes as follows:

> And I firmly believe that nature brings solace for every trouble.
>
> Oh who knows, it won't be long before I can share this overwhelming happiness with *someone* who thinks the way I do about it. (translated edited version)

As you can see, the person who might share her happiness has been changed from "Peter" to "someone" (*iemand*).

In the diary version it is followed by a long "P.S." to Peter, which is a very beautiful and emotional piece of writing, but in the edited version it has been deleted altogether.[1]

*****

The published C-version contains many passages in which Anne describes a truly passionate romantic feeling for Peter. These are, without exception, the result of the absence of an *edited* version on those dates and the adoption of the *diary* version. One such example is 19 Feb 44:

> It was not long before it all became too much for me, my head drooped on to my arm, and I sobbed my heart out. The tears streamed down my cheeks and I felt desperately

---

[1] A shortened version of the P.S. appears in the C-version.

unhappy. Oh, if only "he" had come to comfort me. It was four o'clock by the time I went upstairs again. I went for some potatoes, with fresh hope in my heart of a meeting, but while I was still smartening up my hair in the bathroom, he went down to see Boche in the warehouse.

Suddenly I felt the tears coming back and I hurried to the lavatory, quickly grabbing a pocket mirror as I passed. There I sat then, fully dressed, while the tears made dark spots on the red of my apron, and I felt very wretched.

This is what was going through my mind. Oh, I'll never reach Peter like this. Who knows, perhaps he doesn't like me at all and doesn't need anyone to confide in. Perhaps he only thinks about me in a casual sort of way. I shall have to go on alone once more, without friendship and without Peter. Perhaps soon I'll be without hope, without comfort, or anything to look forward to again. Oh, if I could nestle my head against his shoulder and not feel so hopelessly alone and deserted! Who knows, perhaps he doesn't care about me at all and looks at the others in just the same way. Perhaps I only imagined that it was especially for me? Oh, Peter, if only you could see or hear me. (C-version)

Other entries similarly describe Anne's ardent attachment to Peter. I will enumerate these descriptions in chronological order:

27 Feb 44
From early in the morning till late at night, I really do hardly anything else but think of Peter. I sleep with his image before my eyes, dream about him and he is still looking at me when I awake.

28 Feb 44
It is becoming a bad dream—in daytime as well as at night. I see him nearly all the time and can't get at him, I mustn't show anything, must remain gay while I'm really in des-

pair. Peter Wessel [Schiff] and Peter Van Daan [Pels] have grown into one Peter, who is beloved and good, and for whom I long desperately.

4 Mar 44

From morn till night I look forward to seeing Peter.

6 Mar 44

Oh, Peter, if only I could help you, if only you would let me! Together we could drive away your loneliness and mine! …

P.S. You know I honestly write to you about everything, and so I have to tell you that I'm actually living life from one encounter with him to another. I always hope to discover that he is also waiting for me in the same way, and I am delighted within myself when I notice his small, shy attempts. He would like oh so much, I think, to be able to say as much as I do; he also doesn't know that it is his awkwardness that strikes me so.[2]

These are all present in the published version in both the Dutch and the Japanese. Since the edited version does not exist on this date, the description in the diary version is used as is.

However, on the next day, 7 March, both the diary version and the edited B-version are present:

After New Year the second big change, my dream ..... with that *I discovered Peter*, discovered a second equally heavy struggle beside me, discovered my desire for a boy; not for a girl friend, but for a boy friend. Also discovered the happiness in myself and my armor of superficiality and cheerfulness. But at times I became silent. *Now I live only for*

---

[2] Added to the A-version: "Oh sweetheart! (it sounds so banal, but it's not at all!)"

Peter, because very much will depend on him, on what will happen to me next! (A-version)

Na Nieuwjaar de tweede grote verandering, m'n droom ..... *daarmee ontdekte ik Peter, ontdekte een tweede even zware* *strijd naast me, ontdekte m'n verlangen naar een jongen;* *niet naar een meisjesvriendin, maar naar een jongens-* *vriend. Ontdekte ook het geluk in mezelf en m'n pantser* *van oppervlakkig- en vrolijkheid. Maar bij tijd en wijle* *werd ik stil. Nu leef ik alleen nog maar op Peter, want van* *hem zal zeer veel afhangen, van wat er met mij verder zal* *gebeuren!* (A-version)

This is the description of the diary version. In the edited B-version of the same day, it reads as follows:

After New Year's the second big change, my dream .... and with it I discovered my limitless desire for all that is beautiful and good.

Na Nieuwjaar de tweede grote verandering, m'n droom .... *daarmee ontdekte ik m'n grenzenlozet verlangen naar alles* *wat mooi en goed is.*

As you can see, the description of her romance with Peter has been completely removed.

The most extreme example of such "editing to remove Peter" can be found in the subsequent dates 11 and 12 March. First, I will quote the diary A-version in succession:

11 Mar 44
Lately I can't seem to still; I walk from top to bottom and from bottom to top again. I sometimes have moods that I need to be alone or at least with Peter…

12 Mar 44

Everything is getting crazier and crazier since yesterday Peter doesn't look at me. It is as if he is angry with me, so now I am trying very hard not to follow him and to talk to him as little as possible, but it is very difficult! What could it be that often keeps him away from me and often sends him to me? Maybe I am imagining that it is worse than it really is, maybe he too has moods, maybe tomorrow everything will be fine again!

The hardest thing of all, when I'm so down and sad, is to keep my normal appearance. I have to talk, help, sit together and most of all I have to be cheerful! Most of all I miss Nature and one little place where I can be alone for as long as I want! I think I am mixing up all kinds of things, Kitty, but I am also completely confused:

Day and night, always when I'm awake I do nothing but wonder, "Didn't you leave him alone enough? Are you upstairs too much? Do you talk too much about serious things that he can't talk about yet? Does he perhaps not find you sympathetic at all? Was the whole to-do just imagination? But then why did he tell you so much about himself? Does he perhaps regret that?" And a whole lot more. ...

Ordinary people, ordinary girls, and teenage girls like me will think I am crazy, but no one knows the pain of being in one-sided love and always being around the person you adore. For nothing in the world would I want to miss Peter, yet I would love to be completely away from him one day. This is crazy, but also understandable, because when I just bring some order to my thoughts and feelings in an hour of work, I see him again and all good intentions are destroyed in a single beat.

I am unhappy in love, countless suitors and youngsters have begged for my favors, while I felt nothing but camaraderie for them. But three have been ones I have loved and none of them found anything about me.

Oh Peter, say something at last, don't let me drift between hope and dejection any longer. Give me a kiss or
send me out of the room, but that way I commit an accident. The sweetest scenes in the evening, the barest reality
in the morning, and for weeks on end, every day, I am not
strong enough for that! ...

Moreover, I would not be able to see many people all
day, that someone knows what is going on in me, my trusted one cannot be around me all day, except for ... Peter!

As mentioned above, the diary version 11 March is reflected in the edited
B-version of 12 March. The first part is quoted here. Please read it carefully, noting the differences with the diary version:

I can't seem to sit still lately; I run upstairs and down and
then back again. I love talking to Peter, but I'm always
afraid of being a nuisance. He has told me a bit about the
past, about his parents and about himself. It's not half
enough though and I ask myself why it is that I always long
for more. He used to think I was unbearable; and I returned
the compliment; now I have changed my opinion, has he
changed his too?

I think so; still it doesn't necessarily mean that we shall
become great friends, although as far as I am concerned, it
would make the time here much more bearable.

But still, *I won't get myself upset about it* - I see quite a
lot of him and there's no need to make you unhappy about
it too, kitty, just because I feel so miserable.

In the edited version, the story about Peter ends here, although the entry
itself goes on for quite a while after this, moving on to the relationship
between Anne and Margot. The diary version 12 March has the same
date, but most of it has been deleted. In the English version, 12 March,
only the edited version is retained, and all the contents of the diary version are omitted.

The difference in Anne's love feeling for Peter between the two versions is astonishing. In the edited version, Peter's value to Anne has been downgraded to "a good friend who makes her life better" at best. And she's very calm about it.

If we list the statements in the diary version again, it is hard to believe that they were written by the same person:

- "Oh, if only 'he' had come to comfort me."
- "Now I live only on Peter, because very much will depend on him, on what will happen to me next!"
- "[O]n the one hand I am mad with desire for him, I can hardly be in the room without looking at him, and on the other hand I wonder why I care so much about him, why I don't care enough about myself, why I can't calm down again!"
- "Oh Peter, say something at last, don't let me drift between hope and dejection any longer. Give me a kiss or send me out of the room"
- "It is becoming a bad dream—in daytime as well as at: night. I see him nearly all the time and can't get at him"
- "Oh, Peter, if only you could see or hear me."

It is as if Anne has become a "dual personality".

Ironically, this expression is actually present in the last entry, 1 Aug 44 ("I have already told you that I have, as it were, a dual personality.") To me, this feels like an excuse for the loss of consistency in Anne's romantic feelings as a result of the editing. In the first place, if we go back to the principle as a diary, rewriting the emotions that occurred in the author's mind is clearly beyond the acceptable range of editing.

However, if this problem is excluded, the following counterarguments are possible:

> "The mind of an adolescent girl is changeable. In fact, in the entry of 15 Jul 44, Anne is disappointed in Peter and wants to end the relationship. That's why Anne rewrote her overly passionate description for publication. "

However, this is also questionable. Because, as mentioned above, not all such entries have been rewritten. As a result, Anne's emotions are terribly incoherent if we only read the published version.

Personally, I feel that this bizarre editing severely undermines the value of the book not only as a diary but also as a purely literary work. Furthermore, emotional inconsistency does not only occur between the diary version and the edited version. Even if we limit it to the diary version, it is already there.

In the entry of 22 Mar 44, only ten days after the entry of 12 March mentioned above, she wrote about the letter she sent to Margot. Somehow, Anne transcribed the entire text of the letter Margot replied to in her diary. Why didn't she just paste the actual letter? Moreover, the actual letter has not been found. Be that as it may, there are some very interesting statements in this afterwards:

> All that joke of marrying Peter if we stay here for a long time was not so crazy. I don't think about marrying him, I don't know how he will become when he is an adult, I don't know if we will love each other so much that we would like to get married.
>
> That Peter also loves me I am now sure, in what way that love is I do not know. (A-version)

Since this is a diary version, she must not have "hidden her true feelings" in case anyone would read it.

When did Anne turn into a person with such a boring mindset as "I don't know if we will ever love each other in the future"? Isn't this a dispassionate opinion, as if she were a third person observing their relationship? Peter and Anne kiss for the first time on 15 Apr 44, a later date than this. In general terms, isn't 12 March the time when the love affair is at its most intense?

In response to this, an enthusiastic fan might argue as follows:

> "No, we can read from this text that Anne had a duality. On
> the one hand, she wrote passionately about love, and on the
> other hand, she had a very realistic view of marriage."

Unfortunately, this view is also highly questionable. There is the other entry that reveals Anne's view of marriage before this one. The last part of the diary version 6 Jan 44 reads as follows:

> A week ago, even yesterday, if anyone had asked me,
> "Which of your friends do you consider would be the most
> suitable to marry?" I would have answered, "Sally [a boy],
> because with him it is good, quiet and safe!"; but now I
> would cry, "Petel, because I love him with all my heart and
> soul. I give myself completely!" But one thing, he may
> touch my face, but no more.

Sally seems to be the boy that Anne fell in love with when she was in kindergarten. And Petel, whose name is, oddly, only one letter different from 'Peter,' is another boy that Anne liked when she moved to the "hideout". Why didn't she consider at that time the question of what kind of men they would be when they grew up and whether or not her love for them would last into the future? However, it would be more natural for an ordinary fourteen-year-old girl to have such an innocent longing to marry a boy she likes in the future.

But even though she wrote, "Petel and Peter have grown into one Peter, who is beloved and good, and for whom I long desperately," she also wrote, "I'm not thinking of marrying him". Why on earth is this?

If we try to imagine the situation she was in and the state of mind she was in, the unnaturalness of Anne's opinion as if she were a bystander that she allegedly wrote on 22 Mar 44 becomes even more apparent. The people in the "hideout" seemed to be living in despair. Their daily rations were stagnant, and they could not step out of the "hideout". Conversations had to be conducted in hushed tones. They were not allowed to make a single sound. Tomorrow, or even the next moment, the police might find the "hideout" and take Anne and the others to the camps.

Then, what awaited them would be "gassing". At least that's what Anne thought, and she was "terrified".

What can an adolescent girl who is in such a situation find in her heart? What else could it be but a boy she is in love with?

If we follow Anne's set of circumstances, wouldn't the romantic feelings previously described in the diary version be completely natural? On the contrary, the statement "I don't know how he will be when he grows up, I don't know if we will ever love each other so much that we would like to get married" on 22 Mar 42 is extremely unnatural.

At this point, did they have any hope of getting out of the "hideout"? When would the war end? When would the horror of gas executions be over? She didn't even know if she would be able to live "tomorrow", let alone "in the future". Why would Anne, who wanted to marry Sally or Petel, not want to marry Peter (who was identical to Petel) right now?

Why is she laid back and envisioning "changes in emotions after becoming an adult"?

An Accidental Narrative Plot?

I should like to point out the problem of story structure in relation to the period of writing the Diary.

Above I have already mentioned that Anne's romantic feeling for Peter is inconsistent and unnatural. It is also very strange that it starts in January 1944, 18 months after the start of the "hideout" life in July 1942. If Anne was a very immature girl and only became interested in love around January 1944, this would not be unnatural. But Anne must have been rather precocious in love, because when she was in kindergarten, she liked a boy called Sally, whom she wanted to marry in the future. From the early days of her diary, she was very interested in boys her own age, particularly in relation to her boyfriend, Hello.

However, as soon as she starts living in the "hideout", Anne stops writing about anything romantic. She even stops mentioning Petel, whom she used to love. Given the desperate situation she was supposedly in, wouldn't her feelings for Petel, her only source of emotional support, only become purer and stronger? Then, for no apparent reason at all, a year and a half later, the feverish longing for Petel suddenly returns. At the same time, the overlapping presence of Petel brings Anne closer to Peter, who, when they first met, had a dismal reputation as a "gawky youth" or "can't expect much from his company". The reason for this strange dormancy and sudden resurrection of the romantic feeling can be clearly understood by introducing the concept of story structure into the Diary.

*****

Let us analyze the structure of the Diary in terms of the number of pages. The Japanese version of Anne's Diary has 569 pages.

On p. 50 (about 9% from the beginning), Anne and her family move into the "hideout" and the entrance is camouflaged by a book shelf. The romance with Peter begins on p. 267 (about 47%). It is on p. 425 (75%) that the "hideout" is in "the greatest danger" when thieves and policemen enter the house. Peter and Anne kiss on p. 448 (about 79%). The beginning is when the Frank and Pels families enter the "hideout", followed by the various Midway episodes in which the characters unfold. The main attraction of the story is the romance between Anne and Peter, which comes in the second half. It is on p. 527 (about 93%) that their love begins to decline. It is only just before the end, on p. 555 (about 98%), that Anne decides to reassess her relationship with Peter. And the final entry, 1 Aug 44, is a fitting end to the book's story. It is a truly moving piece of writing that leaves a lingering impression on the reader and hints at her subsequent fate.

In this way, you can see that the episodes are arranged in a very balanced way throughout the Diary. Anne is supposed to have started writing a great deal of text from 12 Jun 42, as if the dike had burst, even though she had never written a good deal of text before. It seems that her "hideout" life started right after that, by accident. And the whole episode is arranged so that the events leading up to 4 Aug 44, when the Franks are taken away, just happen to be the end of the whole story.

It is quite difficult to believe that these are all coincidences. It is often said that there are no coincidences in history. But suppose that their "hideout" life had coincidentally lasted another year or two longer. Furthermore, let's assume that the war ends with the collapse of the Nazi regime and everyone is free from the "hideout". Imagine that, as a result, the Diary became twice as long as it is known today. What would have happened to the contents of the Diary? How could a love affair with Peter, which turned sour just three months after they kissed, have gone on for five hundred pages without any other special event? It would have made for a very redundant and uncomfortable drama. Clearly, Anne's Diary would not be a beautiful composition if it did not end with the entry 1 Aug 44.

However, Anne could not have known the day she would be taken away, the day the Diary would come to an end. So there is good reason to suppose that the text of all the diaries is a story composed by someone else after she was taken away.

Applying this concept of story structure highlights how Anne's feelings for Peter were adjusted and modified.

Why is there no mention of romance in the first half of life in the 'hideout'? The reason for this is simply to place the romance with Peter, the highlight of the drama, in the second half of the drama. The sudden revival of Anne's long-forgotten love for Petel is merely a theatrical convenience, linking it to her romantic feeling for Peter. (In the first place, the idea of a love affair with Petel overlapping with that of Peter seems like something a scenario writer would come up with.)

As far as I can see, the writer had placed the peak of Anne's romantic feeling at 28 Apr 44, when they kiss. In the context of this plot, Anne's adoration of Peter in the March diary version may have been a little too passionate. The editor may have cut some of the descriptions to make Anne's emotions a bit calmer. However, it seems to me that Anne's romantic feeling is very inconsistent because this adjustment process was done halfway.

So why, near the end of the diary, did Anne decide to reassess her relationship with Peter? As far as I can tell from reading 15 Jul 44, the text on this is very abstract and makes no sense at all. It doesn't seem that she and Peter had any quarrel. In an earlier entry, there was mention of differences between the two religions, but it is hard to see how such a previously known issue could have soured relations in just three short months. And in a "desperate hideout life", a boyfriend would have been the greatest comfort for Anne.

However, considering the concept of Diary as a narrative, this is also obvious. If the diary ends with Anne happy in their relationship, the tragic nature of the fate that awaits her is undermined. Therefore, the author may have placed a sad sentence in the third entry from the end, reminding us of the end of summer.

A Budding Lesbian

Certainly it is normal for an adolescent girl to have conflicting and confusing feelings about her blossoming sexuality. According to recent research, around 15% of all girls in their mid-teens have some thoughts of being either lesbian or bisexual. Anne seems to fall into this category. Consider this remarkable A-text entry from when she was around 14 and a half:

> **6 Jan 44**
>
> [Dutch journalist] Sis Heyster also writes that girls of this age don't feel quite sure of themselves, and discover that they themselves are individuals with ideas, thoughts, and habits. After I came here, when I was scarcely 13, I began to think about myself rather early on and to know that I am a person. Sometimes, when I lie in bed at night, I have a terrible desire to feel my breasts and to listen to the quiet rhythmical beat of my heart.
>
> I already had such feelings subconsciously before I came here, because I remember one night when I slept with Jacque I could not contain myself, I was so curious to see her body, which she always kept hidden from me and which I had never seen. I asked Jacque whether as a proof of our friendship we might feel one another's breasts. Jacque refused. I also had a terrible desire to kiss Jacque and that I did.

> I go into ecstasies every time I see the naked figure of a
> woman, such as Venus in the Springer History of Art, for
> example. It strikes me sometimes as so wonderful and ex-
> quisite that I have difficulty not letting the tears roll down
> my cheeks.
> If only I had a girl friend!

Here, Anne thinks back to the time "before I came here," to what appears
to be a nascent lesbian relationship, one that apparently never developed.
At that time, Anne would have been 11 or 12. And even now, at age 14
and a half, she "wishes she had a girl friend"—presumably for a sexual
(or at least physical) relationship.

Anne's open-ended sexual desire continues to develop. In the A-
version entry for 12 Feb 44, cited above, we read:

> I'm longing—so longing—for everything... I have to keep
> myself under control... I long for every boy...

Apparently Anne has strong bisexual inclinations at this point—if indeed
it is Annelies who is expressing her honest feelings here.

Urinating in Front of a Strange Man?

Another issue often overlooked is the problem of "strange room assignments" for the sake of dramatic convenience.

As you can see in Figure 19, Anne and the dentist, Dussel, sleep in
the same room!—the same, very small room! How is it possible for a 13-
to 15-year-old girl to sleep with another adult male, a stranger, in the
same room? According to the B-text entry of 4 Aug 43, when Anne
needs to go to the bathroom in the middle of the night, she uses the "met-
al pot under my bed", which means she pees right in front of Dussel, who
is sleeping next to her!

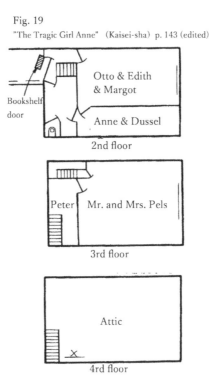

Fig. 19
"The Tragic Girl Anne" (Kaisei-sha) p. 143 (edited)

On the other hand, Mr. and Mrs. Frank and Margot are in the same room. I can't help but think that this room assignment is insane and crazy. At the very least, it would be normal to assign these two rooms as a "men's room" (Otto and Dussel) and a "women's room" (Anne, Margot, and mother Edith).

However, there was clearly another way to completely solve the overcrowding problem in the "hideout"—utilize the attic, which was the largest area in the "hideout", but for some reason no one was using it. A bed should have been brought in and this attic should have been used by Dussel, a stranger to the Pels and Frank families, as his room, or at least when he went to bed. The 3rd floor is used by the Pels. And if Otto and his wife use one of the two rooms on the 2nd floor, and Anne and Margot use the other, all problems are solved. This would have been the most ideal and sensible room assignment. Why didn't anyone in the "hideout" adopt this very simple solution? Why did everyone leave the large attic unattended and let Anne and Dussel sleep in the same room—an "impossible situation," in Anne's words? In many related books, the existence of attic is not depicted as a diagram, so most readers are unaware of this absurdity.

Of course, common sense alone is not enough to solve this difficult problem. However, if you consider the "convenience of drama," the purpose of this measure is obvious. If the attic is not left unattended, there will be no place for Anne and Peter to interact. After 6 Jan 44, Anne "somehow got the idea to talk to Peter," and since that time, the attic is often used as a place where Anne and Peter deepen their friendship. If the only place they could be alone in the hideout was Peter's small room, it would have been inconvenient for the story structure.

Writing a Blue Story in the Presence of Seven People?

Finally, we turn to a handful of truly amazing entries. These are the best examples of proof for the argument that Annelies did not write these entries herself. In these, Anne offers incredibly-detailed commentary on her own genitalia.

The first of these is an A-version text of 28 Sep 42:

> Dearest Pien,
> I use a preserving glass as a potty, it's in the bathroom during the day but I am horribly afraid that they might want to use it as a preserving glass again, but just smelling it should be more than enough for them. At night I manage it all by feeling and I put it right round my "vagina" and a little bit further round it works all right.

> *Beste Pien,*
> *Als po gebruik ik een wekglas, het staat overdag in de badkamer maar ik ben doodsbenauwd dat ze het nog eens als wekglas willen hebben, maar als ze er aan ruiken zullen ze er wel genoeg aan hebben. 's Nachts doe ik het al op ge-*

voel en ik doe het juist om mijn «vagina» en een eindje eromheen, het gaat best. (A-version)

The next one is 10 Oct 42.

> Dear Kitty,
> My vagina is getting wider all the time, but I could also be imagining it. When I am on the w.c., I sometimes look then I can see quite definitely that the urine comes out of a little hole in the vagina, but above it there is something else, there is a hole in that too, but I don't know what for. (A-version)

> *Beste Kitty,*
> *Mijn vagina wordt steeds wijderd, maar het kan ook dat ik me dat verbeeld. Als ik op de w.c. ben, kijk ik er wel eens naar en dan zie ik heel stellig, dat het urine uit een gaatje in de vagina komt, maar er boven zit ook nog een ding, daar is ook een gat in, maar ik weet niet waar voor dat dient.* (A-version)

Then we jump ahead to 24 Jan 44, when Anne is having a discussion with Peter about the gender of their cat, Boche:

> Peter: "Tell me, how do you say '*geschlectsteil*' ['sex organ,' in German] in Dutch?"
> Anne: "*Geslachtsdeel.*"
> "No, that's not what I mean."
> "Oh, you mean the other thing, I don't know the word." …
> "Peter, a *geschlechtsteil* is a *geslachtsdeel*, and it has a different name in male and female animals."
> "I know that."
> "In females it is called a vagina, I know that much, but I don't know what it's called in males."

This may come as a surprise to many people, to say the least. These comments have all been rejected in the foreign published versions as a matter of course. The third entry, however, appears in the Japanese edition, which claims to be the complete version. And the following from the diary version 24 Mar 44, is also rejected in the English version but present in the Japanese version:

> I wanted to ask him if he knows what a girl actually looks like there. I don't think that a boy is as complicated down there than a girl. You can see exactly what a naked man looks like from photographs or pictures, but you can't with women. With them, the sexual parts or whatever they are called are further between the legs. (A-version; RCE p. 588)

> *Ik wou hem vragen of hij wel weet hoe een meisje er eigenlijk uitziet. Een jongen is van beneden geloof ik niet zo ingewikkeld ingericht dan een meisje. Op foto's of afbeelden van naakte mannen kun je toch heel goed zien hoe die eruit zien, maar bij vrouwen niet. Daar zitten de geslachtsdelen of hoe dat heet wel meer tussen de benen.* (diary version)

Later in the same entry, she adds:

> [B]efore I was 11 or 12 years old I didn't realize that there were two inner lips as well, you couldn't see them at all. And the funniest thing of all was that I thought that urine came out of the clitoris.

This is remarkably graphic for a young girl, writing in difficult situations, in cramped quarters amidst family and strangers. And yet the entry for 24 March continues:

> From the front when you stand up you can see nothing but hair, between your legs there are things like little cushions,

soft, with hair on too, which press together when you stand up so that you can't see what's inside. When you sit down they divide and inside it looks very red and ugly and fleshy. At the very top, between the big outer lips there is a little fold of skin which turns out to be a kind of little bladder on closer inspection, that is the clitoris. Then come the small inner lips, they are also pressed against each other just like a little pleat. When they open, there is a fleshy little stump inside, no bigger than the top of my thumb. The top of it is porous, there are different little holes in it and that's where the urine comes out. The lower part looks as if it's nothing but skin, but that's where the vagina is. There are little folds of skin all over the place, you can hardly find it.

The little hole underneath is so terribly small that I simply can't imagine how a man can get in there, let alone how a whole baby can get out. The hole is so small that you can't even put your index finger in, not easily anyway. That's all it is and yet it plays such an important role!

So now we are in biology class! And Dr. Frank is explaining to us the minute details of female anatomy. Needless to say, none of this appears in the B- or C-versions.

To assume that Annelies wrote these descriptions is puzzling on at least two counts. First, she consistently and very clearly refers to the entire female genitalia as "vagina" three times. In particular, in the third statement, she clearly says to Peter, a boy, "The female's is called the vagina". But in the fourth entry, for some reason, she writes "the genitals or whatever they are called" and muddies the name. On the other hand, in this entry, she clearly mentions words like "labia" (*schaamlippen*), "clitoris" (*kittelaar*), and "cunnus" (*scheede*), which is even stranger. It would make sense if this was a "mistake" by a different author than Annelies, who did not remember his own previous writings.

The other problem is more fundamental. According to the official setting, Anne's private room did not exist in the "hideout". There was nowhere she could lock herself in and be alone. And it seemed that there were always seven other people living in the small "hideout". The only attic was unoccupied, but even there it was adjacent to Peter's room downstairs, separated by a single door.

In the diary version, between 20 and 22 Mar 44, there is an entry without a date titled "Anne's Time Schedule", which describes the time schedule in detail. It says, "From 10:30 a.m. to 12:00 a.m., I study, write in my diary, or spend time in idleness". After that, "from 12:00 to 15:00 a.m., I go to the attic to enjoy the fresh air". According to this, the diary was not written in the attic, but in the Frank family's area on the third floor. And even if she happens to be able to write her diary alone, she never knows who might read her diary in the small "hideout" at any time.

As we see, the diary version of 24 March goes on to describe, in great detail, the shape of her genitals. Surprisingly, the Japanese edition publishes it all. Imagine, if you can, a 13 to 15-year-old girl describing endlessly the structure of her genitals in a small space inhabited by seven people, including four men.

Now, you can better understand the anomaly of this Diary. I have a very hard time believing that a young girl could write such explicit words in circumstances of virtually no privacy. But I do not have a hard time believing that a middle-aged Jewish man, with a fixation on teen sexuality, could write such words.

CHAPTER 4

BEGINNING AND END OF THE HIDEOUT

The 'Genius Writer' Who Never Wrote Again

The allegation most frequently made about Anne's diary is that it is too well-written and mature to be written by a 13- to 15-year-old girl. Consider this remark by Arthur R. Butz, a professor of electrical engineering at Northwestern University, who was the first person to systematically and unbiasedly study the Holocaust. He, too, wrote about his impressions of Anne's diary; and he said, "I don't believe it".[1]

I am particularly qualified to comment on this matter. This is because my main business is running a tutoring school, and I am rightly involved in the education of boys and girls of the same age as Annelies. In general, teachers change the class or grade they are in charge of every year, so most of the time their relationship with the same student lasts only one year. However, in my case, I have been teaching each of my students for up to six years on a continuous basis, almost as a private tutor. The total number of students is quite large. Therefore, I know firsthand how the average child between the ages of ten and fifteen grows, how fast they grow, and what their writing ability is like. In primary education, the first priority should be to memorize "things that can be practiced repeatedly". This includes learning basic math skills and memorizing knowledge in science, history and geography. The abilities that can be improved in a short period of time through general study are basically limited to these.

In contrast, improvement of fundamental thinking ability and improvement of language ability progress at a very slow pace. These change step by step with physical growth, at least over a period of several

---

[1] In his *Hoax of the Twentieth Century* (2003), Butz wrote "The question of the authenticity of the diary is not considered important enough to consider here [in this book]; I will only remark that I have looked it over and don't believe it" (p. 59).

years. Of these, writing ability is the one that grows at a particularly slow rate. In this age group, boys tend to have relatively lower writing ability than girls, because writing ability is directly related to mental age. Boys are generally mentally younger than girls, and it is not uncommon for a junior high school student to be unable to write a single line of an essay. For such children, the only way is to let them write what they can write at that moment.

The easiest way to get children to write is to have them write about what happened, or the facts themselves. What is more difficult is to write about how they felt. Children can barely write this, but most of the time, they can only describe it in really simple words such as "I had fun," "I was happy," or "It was delicious". The mental world of children at this age is still in its infancy. They are just beginning to add rich colors to their once pure white world. They do not yet have the ability to translate them into a proper language. And the most difficult part is to write a thought. With repeated practice in composition, they too can technically master up to writing a superficially well-formed sentence. However, writing ability is almost equal to mental age, and in the end, nothing more than what exists in the writer's mental world will be born as words. Deep insight into things is not even present in the majority of children to begin with. The growth of writing ability is a process that takes place over a long span of time, at least a few years or even decades, as one matures mentally.

With that in mind, let's read the text of 6 Jul 44 (A-version) as an example:

> I've so often thought how lovely it would be to have some-
> one's complete confidence, but now, now that I'm that far,
> I realize how difficult it is to think what the other person is
> thinking and then to find the right answer. More especially
> because the very ideas of "easy" and "money" are some-
> thing entirely foreign and new to me. Peter's beginning to
> lean on me a bit and that mustn't happen under any circum-
> stances. A type like Peter finds it difficult to stand on his
> own feet, but it's even harder to stand on your own feet as a

conscious, living being. Because if you do, then it's twice as difficult to steer a right path through the sea of problems and still remain constant through it all.

I'm just drifting around, have been searching for days, searching for a good argument against that terrible word "easy," something to settle it once and for all.

How can I make it clear to him that what appears easy and attractive will drag him down into the depths, depths where there is no comfort to be found, no friends and no beauty, depths from which it is almost impossible to raise oneself?

We all live, but we don't know the why or the where-fore. We all live with the object of being happy; our lives are all different and yet the same. We three have been brought up in good circles, we have the chance to learn, the possibility of attaining something, we have all reason to hope for much happiness, but ... we must earn it for our-selves. And that is never easy. You must work and do good, not be lazy and gamble, if you wish to earn happi-ness. Laziness may appear attractive, but work gives satis-faction.

It's not that this part in particular is the only advanced writing. Sentences like this one are ubiquitous in Anne's diary. You may have felt the same way as Professor Butz: "I don't believe it."

In my experience, not a single middle school student has been able to write at the same level as this. In the first place, not everyone, even adults, can write at this level. Of course, I'm not saying that there can't be 15-year-olds with this level of writing talent. But if there is one, she must be extremely talented.

However, Anne's performance in school was only fair if we trust the description of 5 Jul 42, while her sister Margot was very good at school.

In Schnabel's book, mentioned above, there are a number of inter-esting testimonies on this point from people who were involved. For ex-

ample, Mijnheer van G., Annelies' homeroom teacher when she was in
the first grade, said:

> No, I can say only what I have said before: she was no
> prodigy. … She certainly was not an extraordinary child,
> not even ahead of her age. (p. 52)

And Anne's sixth grade teacher, "K," said: "She was still very young for
the class, and very frail also" (p. 53). In contrast, her sister Margot seems
to have been very academically talented and mentally mature. The testimonies about this are in perfect agreement. Kugler, for example, seems
to have had the following impression: "In his opinion, Anne was not as
intelligent as her sister, or at any rate not as mentally developed..." (p.
99). Lies, who was a friend of Annelies, also testified in support of this:

> Anne and I were very close friends, you must understand
> that, and yet no one suspected that she could write. With
> Margot it would have been different. We thought Margot
> terribly talented and capable of anything. But Anne, you
> see, was just my friend… (p. 36)

The mother of Annelies' friend Jopie said:

> Margot was entirely different. You would never imagine
> that two persons could be so very different. Margot was
> always summa cum laude—all through school, all through
> life. She, too, was candid and decided, but she was quiet
> and kind. She was such an exceptional girl that I was al-
> ways speechless with her. But Anne took after her grand-
> mother, and after her Great-aunt Frank. (p. 48)

It should be noted that none of the writings of the hidden genius Annelies
have been identified before she started writing her diary in June 1942. In
fact, on 7 Mar 44, Anne wrote, "In the latter half of 1943…I began to

write stories…", and all the stories attributed to Annelies were written after August 1943, after the start of the diary.

Furthermore, on 7 Aug 43, as mentioned above, it is written that "I started writing a story some weeks ago". Also, as mentioned above, she first wrote about her dream of becoming a writer in her diary on 5Apr 44, that is, almost two years after she started writing her diary. Does this mean that she suddenly wrote such advanced sentences without any experience of writing lengthy texts before her diary? If that is the case, I must say the same thing as Professor Butz: "I don't believe it."

In my long teaching career, I have learned the universal principle that children will only do what they want to do unless they are told to do it by their parents or teachers. This is probably true for most of us adults, but children are even less likely to act according to a sense of duty or purpose.

In my experience, there are very few students who like to study, except for a very few exceptions. Almost all the students belong to one of the following categories: extreme dislike, tolerable or not bad. In the diary, it is never mentioned that she was obliged by anyone to write a diary. Therefore, all the texts were written at the complete free will of the author. For someone who wrote such a large amount of text on a daily basis, she must have definitely loved writing very much. Painters and musicians with a genius background draw pictures and play musical instruments as if they were breathing, every day from an early age. How and when did Anne, a genius writer, develop her talent? As I have already mentioned, the development of writing ability is very slow and gradual. Anne's ability to write like a professional writer at the age of 13 is predicated on a prior period of relative immaturity in her writing.

A fan might say: "Anne created stories from an early age and continued to write at a similar pace, creating illustrated books and fairytales to share with her classmates and family. It would be normal to imagine it that way. However, in reality, her writings and trajectory as a girl writer before the diary are not known at all. However, in Schnabel's book there are interesting testimonies by two women who were adults at the time: Jopie's mother (p. 65) and Mijnheer (p. 74). They both say that Anne was an aspiring and talented writer from an early age."

If this is the case, why are none of Anne's writings from before the diary identified? Why is the first entry that mentions the dream of becoming a writer on 5 Apr 44? I would like to emphasize that the above two women, while saying so, do not at the same time say that they have actually read the stories written by Annelies.

Anne's Missing Letter from Auschwitz

At the same time, it is also extremely unnatural that there are no writings found after the diary. However, I expect most people think, "Anne went to the camps, so she can't possibly have left any writing behind." Such an unconscious assumption is the effect that Anne's diary has had on people around the world.

Why, for example, do we not possess a letter by Anne from Auschwitz? Letters and money could be mailed from Nazi camps. Conversely, outsiders could send all sorts of things to people in the camps. Figure 18 is a postcard from Auschwitz in the possession of Holocaust researcher Carlo Mattogno. On the left side of this postcard, there is a detailed description of the regulations at the camp.[2]

1.) "Every prisoner may receive mail from his family and send it to them twice a month. Letters to prisoners must be clearly legible and written in ink, and may contain only two pages of 15 lines each. Envelopes must be unpadded. A letter may contain no enclosure except a stamp for 6 pfennigs or 12 pfennigs. Everything else is prohibited. Postcards have 10 lines. Photographs may not be used as mail."

2.) "Money may be sent only as postal money orders."

According to this, Annelies had the opportunity to send letters to Miep and others up to four times. Why did Anne, who had been writing so much, suddenly stop writing letters?

---

[2] Carlo Mattogno, *Healthcare in Auschwitz* (2016, p. 32).

Fig. 18 HEALTHCARE IN AUSCHWITZ Carlo Mattogno p. 313

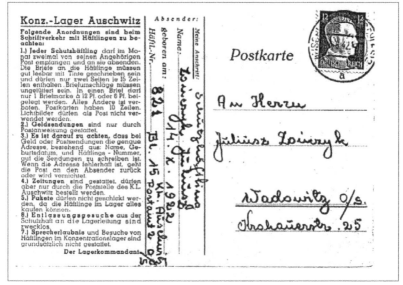

The inmates of the camps were extremely important to the Nazis because they were the labor force for the munitions factories. On 26 October 1943, Oswald Pohl of the SS Economic Management Central Headquarters issued the following order to the camps:

> Not from hypocritical sentimentality, but because we need their arms and legs, because they have to contribute to the German people achieving a great victory. For this we need to take to heart the welfare of the inmates.[3]

And he concludes that the following measures are necessary:

1) A correct and appropriate diet,
2) Correct and appropriate clothing,
3) The use of all natural health resources,

---

[3] Mattogno, ibid., p. 15.

4) Avoiding all unnecessary effort, not directly essential to the ability to work,

5) Productivity bonuses.

The camp labor force was the key to the Nazi war effort. In other words, the Nazis had a compelling motive to prioritize the supply of food and improve the environment because of the camps.

Compare now the food situation in the "hideout." According to the diary, the situation there in 1944 was very tight:

15 Apr 44
There are no vegetables at all. Lettuce before and lettuce after.
Our meals now consist only of potatoes and artificial gravy.

8 May 44
[R]otten potatoes day after day…

5 Jun 44
Very few vegetables and potatoes.

23 Jun 44
We've hardly got any potatoes.

In comparison, the food in the camps was far more substantial.[4] The weekly ration in the camps was:

200g of meat products
100g of cheese
2,600g of rye bread
80g of sugar
2,800g of potatoes
4,000g of fresh vegetables and so on,
for a total of 2,030 kcal per day.

---

[4] http://revisionist.jp/air_photo_evidence/ball_02.htm

In addition, there was no work on Sundays and there was entertainment even on weekdays. There were cinemas, theaters, prisoners' orchestras, boys' choirs, paintings, sculptures and other artistic and cultural activities. There were also sports facilities such as playgrounds and swimming pools.[5] If we follow the description in the diary, the camp was a much more liberal and cultural environment for Anne, who had been confined to a small "hideout" for over two years. Wouldn't it be strange if she didn't report to Miep and the others about her life in the camp, as much as possible?

The Absurdity of "The Beginning"

There is also a great absurdity in the first story of "hideout," which is fundamental to the existence of the diary.

The first part of the 8 Jul 42 entry (A-text) is as follows:

> [A]t about 3 o'clock, a policeman arrived and called from the door downstairs, Miss Margot Frank, Mummy went down and the policeman gave her a card which said that Margot Frank had to report to the S.S.

The call-up notice seems to be about wartime conscription, encouraging people to work at the Westerbork labor and transit camp. In the official RCE (p. 226), the editors add this "explanatory footnote":

> On Saturday 4 July 1942, the Central Office for Jewish Emigration issued the first few thousand call-up notices to Jews. Most of those called up were German Jews and their number included many boys and girls aged from 15 to 18, who had to leave without their parents. The call-up notices were sent by registered post and delivered by the Post Office one day later.

---

[5] Germar Rudolf, *Lectures on the Holocaust* (2005), sec. 4.6.2.

This description in the diary version is quite puzzling in terms of historical facts. As explained in the official version itself, the call-up notice was
to be "mailed by registered post" and not hand-delivered by the police.
So why did Anne record that a "policeman" delivered the note in person?

And worse: The story changes dramatically in the B- and C-
versions. There, it is *Otto* ("Daddy"), not Margot, who is called up! As
we read in the B-text, Margot tells Anne: "The S.S. have sent a call-up
notice for Daddy." So, what is going on? Is the A-text a "mistake"? But
this would be nonsense. Why is it that the diary version, which she wrote
just three days after the call-up notice, when her memory was freshest,
has the wrong description? This absurdity can be explained if we interpret that someone other than Anne wrote the diary version *after the war*,
based on an inaccurate understanding, and then corrected the defects in
the edited versions.

There is also a very important fact related to this call-up notice: the
Frank family wanted to leave the Netherlands and applied to the authorities
to do so. Figure 20 is the registration certificate of the Frank family issued
by the "Central Reich Office for Jewish Emigration". In addition, Figure
21 is the application form for the registration of Otto's company, Pectacon.

Fig. 20　　　　　　　　　　　Fig. 21

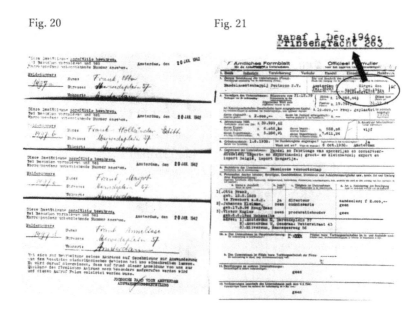

The oval in the upper right corner of the latter clearly shows the address of Otto's company, today the Anne Frank House. This meant that the authorities *knew* that the Frank family was Jewish, *knew* their family home address, and hence the address of the "hideout". That is why the call-up notice was sent to the Frank family by "registered mail"! In the diary, it says that if their existence were known to Germany, they would be immediately taken to the camps. But that's not possible. If the police had intended to arrest the Frank family on the day the call-up notice was received, they could have visited the house that day and detained Anne and the others. In that case, Anne's diary would have ended before it even began!

*****

Inexplicably, in a life that lasted 25 months, there are some statements not in the diary that clearly should be there.

The first is about the fact that the Frank family had applied for immigration, as mentioned above. In the mid-1930s, Hermann Göring summarized the basic principles of National Socialist policy as follows: "The emigration of Jews should be facilitated by all means." The basic policy of the Nazis was to "emigrate" or "evacuate" or "expel" all Jews, first from Germany, then from Europe. It is estimated that 90% of the Jewish population in the Netherlands emigrated after the German invasion of that nation in May 1940. At this point, if the Frank family had also emigrated to the United States or other countries as the Nazis wanted, they obviously would not have been sent to the camps. The text of the diary does not explain how much hope the Frank family had to emigrate, or what circumstances prevented them from doing so, if they had any hope at all. It is extremely puzzling that there is no mention of this issue, because if they had emigrated, they would not have had to live in fear every day.

The second description that should exist but doesn't is the German search for them. If the Nazis had wanted to find the Frank family after they moved into the "hideout", the first place they would have gone would have been the company office building. At the start, the police would have gone to the front office and asked the employees, Miep and others, where Otto and his family were. The police would also have noticed that there was an annex behind the front house, as a matter of course. However, there is no description of a police visit to the company in the diary, even though the entry for 11 Apr 44 describes the police invasion as "the worst crisis of the hideout".

A fact little known to the general public is that the Nazi camps were run by a very Germanic and strict rule of law. For example, a Polish man, K. J., was charged with breach of contract when he returned to work three days late from vacation. He was sent to Auschwitz and other camps for this, and was released after ten weeks.[6]

Also, not all Jews and Gypsies were randomly sent to camps or subjected to forced emigration. Even Gypsies who had regular jobs were not sent to camps.[7] Only a quarter of French Jews who were not French citizens were eligible for transfer; a high percentage of Jews living in the Netherlands, such as the Frank family, were transferred, but were still only 70 percent of the total.[8]

Given that the Frank family was transported to the camps, there must have been a clear legal basis for it (whether or not it was morally right, according to our modern values), but for some reason this point is obscured. To reiterate an important point, the authorities knew that the Franks were Jewish, and they knew the address of their family home and the "hideout". What is certain is that, in any case, the Franks were transferred to the camp on 4 Aug 44. The reason for this must be that there was a legal basis for their internment at that time, and the decision was made to intern them. The reason they were not transferred before that could *never* have been because they lived in a "hideout" and could not be found. Ironically, the fact that the diary does not mention a single word about the police search of the office is consistent with this. The fact that Margot received a call-up notice to the labor camp in 1942 and the Frank family was taken away in 1944 are clearly unrelated.

---

[6] Mattogno, op. cit., p. 41.

[7] Jurgen Graf, *National Socialist Concentration Camps*.

[8] Jurgen Graf, *Holocaust Revisionism and its Political Consequences*, chapter 6.

And as a side note, in his aforementioned book, Schnabel presents an interesting testimony by Mrs. L, the mother of Annelies' friend Trees: "One day Anne and Margot were visiting us and said they might report to the Westerbork work camp" (p. 74). When did this episode take place? Isn't this around the time Margot was old enough to be subject to commandeering, and after she received her call-up notice? Doesn't Mrs. L's testimony also confirm that Anne and her family were *not* living in the "hideout" at the time?

The End of "Hideout": Did the Infamous Bookshelf Door Ever Exist?

Next, let's consider the absurdity of the final story of the "hideout" life, which is fundamental to the existence of diary.

There is conflicting information about what happened when the police came to Otto's office on 4 August 1944. In a letter to Schnabel, Kugler, who oversaw the company, wrote the following:

> At the end of the corridor they all drew their revolvers at once, and the sergeant ordered me to push aside the bookshelf at the end wall of the corridor and open the door behind it.
>
> I said: But there is only a bookcase there! Then he got angry, because he knew everything, and grabbed the bookcase and pulled it himself, and it gave way, and the secret door became visible, perhaps that the hook had not been hooked properly. They opened the door, and I had to go ahead, up the stairs, and the policemen followed me, and I felt their guns in my back. (RCE, p. 22)

The other party to this incident was Karl Josef Silberbauer, a national police officer. He was also interrogated in 1963-64. However, there is a serious discrepancy between Silberbauer's statement and Kugler's letter, as follows. The first statement was made on 25 November 1963:

Since denying this fact seemed futile to the man, he led us up a staircase one floor higher into a small room. When we entered the room, we saw a dresser or a set of shelves on the opposite wall. To the right of it was a window. The head of the company pointed to the piece of furniture. This was then pushed aside, exposing another staircase leading to the upper floor. With my pistol drawn, I went up the stairs with the Crb. (RCE, p. 37)

Silberbauer's second statement is from 4 March 1964:

The head of the company [...] immediately became terribly nervous and all red in the face. Without any pressure [...] not even a single pistol was drawn, the man immediately got up and led us to the hiding place of the Frank family [...]. He also opened the hidden door voluntarily. (RCE, p. 37)

First, according to Kugler, the police walked up to the door of the "hideout" and explicitly said "push aside the bookshelf (*bücherregal*) at the end wall of the corridor and open the door behind it."

On the other hand, according to Silberbauer, Kugler personally led the police to the "hideout" and pointed to a piece of furniture (*Mö-belstück*) on the far wall. Silberbauer identifies the furniture as "a dresser (*Kredenz*) or a set of shelves (*Stellage*)."

Again, the answer to why and where this discrepancy arose can be found in the official version:

21 Aug 42
Mr. Kugler was afraid that they might come here to look for hidden bicycles, and that's why he wanted the door to our hiding place camouflaged, and now they had done it in such a way that it looks like an ordinary bookcase, when in fact it is a door, for the bookcase with all its books swings on hinges so you can open it like a door... (A-version)

Kugler was bang dat ze misschien hier komen om naar ver-
stopte fietsen te kijken, en daarom wilde hij dat de deur
naar ons verblijf gekamoufleerd werd, nu hebben ze het zo
gedaan, dat het er net uitziet alsof het een stellage met
boeken is, maar in werkelijkheid is het een deur, want de
kast zit met boeken en al aan scharnieren vast en zo kun je
het als een deur openmaken…

However, the edited version of the same day says the following:

Mr. Kugler thought it would be better to put a cupboard in
front of our door, (because a lot of houses are being
searched for hidden bicycles.) but, of course, it had to be a
movable cupboard that can open like a door. (B-version)

Mijnheer Kugler vond het n.l. beter om voor onze toe-
gangsdeur een kast te plaatsen, (omdat er veel huis-
zoekingen voor verstopte fietsen gehouden worden.) maar
dan natuurlijk een kast die draaibaar is en die dan als een
deur opengaat.

In Dutch, '*boekenkast*' would clearly mean "bookshelf", but when the
word '*kast*' is used only, as in this sentence, it is not clear what kind of
furniture it is exactly. The word '*kast*' is a general term for furniture of
various shapes and purposes, such as 'cupboard,' 'closet,' or 'shelf.' The
problem here is that the Dutch version, published for the general public,
only contains the text of the latter edited version. And because the English version is edited from the Dutch version, this '*kast*' has been translated into English as "cupboard". This probably means that the majority
of readers of Anne's diary around the world recognize the famous secret
door as a 'cupboard'. In the diary version, however, it is unquestionably
described as "bookcase" (*stellage met boeken*).

More to the point, the existing secret door to the Anne Frank House
is a "bookshelf" clearly lined with books. In every sense of the word, the
swinging door in Anne's Official diary is a definite "bookshelf". Interest-

ingly, in the Japanese version, the original word '*kast*' is consistently translated as "bookshelf", probably because the translator is familiar with the original text. However, Silberbauer calls it by the ambiguous expression "cupboard (*Kredenz*) or shelf (*Stellage*)" or by the generic name "furniture" (*Möbelstück*). He probably did not know the official setting. And he did not see the object as it was. If what was written in the diary was true, there must have been books on the bookshelf at that time. If the state of the bookshelf had been changed, it would have been a hint that there was a secret inhabitant. Check the photos of the existing swinging doors in Figure 22.

The bookshelf door as it exists today was rebuilt after the building was opened to the public as a museum in 1960, an obvious fact that cannot be disputed. Since Otto and others involved in the house survived, if the restoration was done under their supervision, the basic structure would obviously have been the same as during the war. Nevertheless, it is highly doubtful that the state of this door matches the description in the diary. This is because the text of the diary does not confirm that the door is double. Indeed, in the edited version 21 Aug 42, it says "put a cupboard (*kast*) in front of our door (*toegangsdeur*)". However, this itself does not match the rest of the text in the diary:

- As mentioned above, the diary version 21 Aug 42 says that the shelf (*kast*) itself is a door (*deur*).
- The edited version 10 Aug 43 says "*kastdeur*" i.e. "shelf-door", which means "door is the shelf itself".
- The edited version 11 Apr 44 says "the door to the landing was closed, the shelf-door shut" to prevent thieves from entering. Considering the order in which they were closed, "the door to the landing" is the "door from the front house to the landing" across from the "shelf-door". There is no mention of the other original door behind the "shelf-door".

Fig. 22

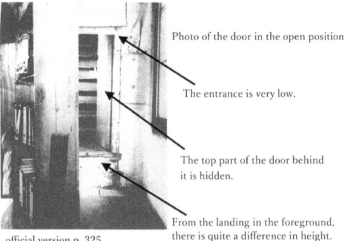

Photo of the door in the open position

The entrance is very low.

The top part of the door behind it is hidden.

official version p. 325.

From the landing in the foreground, there is quite a difference in height.

Photo of the door in closed position.

According to the "diary edition," the books were placed like this.

"Anne Frank, the Tragic Girl" (Kaisei-sha)

- The diary version 15 Oct 42 describes an episode in which a carpenter worked in front of the "hideout". At this point, Anne and Otto went just inside the door (*deur*) and listened closely to find out what was going on. And it says, "The door (*deur*) could not be opened because the hook (*haak*) of the door (*deur*) would not come off." In the edited version 20 Oct 42, which contains the same episode, it says that the hooks (*haak*) of the "shelf-door" (*deur-kast* and *kastdeur*) could not be released, so the shelf (*kast*) could not be opened. These descriptions do not confirm that there is a door behind the "shelf-door" (*kastdeur*).

- On 8 Jul 44, it says "Pete tore upstairs, locked the shelf-door (*kastdeur*)" because the doorbell at the entrance rang. If the original door was also inside, it should be possible to lock it as well. However, there is no mention of it.

Thus, the other original door behind the "shelf-door" is not present in the text of the diary. However, in the current situation, in the Anne Frank House today, there is indeed a door behind the "shelf-door," and Kugler's letter is perfectly consistent with this.

*****

To add to this, a crucial discrepancy needs to be mentioned. According to Kugler, the police were all armed with pistols before entering the "hideout" and opened the " bookshelf door" themselves. On the other hand, according to Silberbauer, Kugler himself led the way to the "hideout" and it was he who opened the door. It was only after he had entered the room that the police raised their pistols. These can be summarized as follows:

Kugler's letter:
- The police knew about the "hideout", about the "shelf door" and about the door behind it.
- The police called the shelf a "bookshelf".
- The police were the ones who went to the "hideout" and opened the "bookshelf door".
- The bookshelf door was pulled open and there was another door behind it.
- The police all had their pistols at the ready even before they opened the door.

Silberbauer's statement:
- The police did not know the location of the "hideout" or the "shelf door".
- He perceives the shelf as "furniture" like a "cupboard".
- It was Kugler himself who led the way to the "hideout" and opened the "shelf door".
- He pushed open the "shelf door" and a staircase appeared.
- After entering the "hideout", the police raised their pistols.

When listed in this way, the two disagree on all points.

*****

Another interview with Silberbauer was conducted by a Dutch journalist of *The Hague Post*, apart from the interrogation statement by the Dutch authorities. According to this, he does not explain in detail how the police entered the "hideout", which is the most important point (see Faurisson report, sec. 70).

According to Faurisson, this witness is "an honest man who has retained a good memory of those days". He strongly wished to remain anonymous, so his real name and address have been sealed inside an envelope by Faurisson. It is not clear what connection this person had with the case, but my guess is that he was probably one of the eight officers who investigated. He said that when the police arrived at the building they went straight to the annex without being told by anyone. The entrance to the "hideout" did not have a door in the shape of a shelf, but only a solid wooden door (original word: *ein Holzverschlag*).

Thus, there are *three* different accounts of the entrance door to the "hideout":

1) There were two doors: a bookshelf door, which could be opened by pulling, and a normal door inside, which could be opened by pushing.
2) There was one "furniture door", which could be opened by pushing.
3) There was one "normal door", which could be opened by pushing.

Common sense tells us that the truth is one of these three, and that the other two are false. From the official point of view, the testimony of the anonymous person in (3) cannot be trusted. However, (1) and (2) disagree at every turn, and at least one of them is certain to be wrong. Then we should never rule out the possibility that (3) is correct and (1) and (2) are both wrong, i.e. that there was no such thing as a shelf door.

In fact, Schnabel visited the building after the war, and he did *not* see any "shelf door" on that occasion. He says "nothing is left but the twisted hinges hanging beside the door" (p. 85), without saying whether an ordinary door existed or not. Therefore, the possibility that the "hinges" were left behind after the original door was removed should be considered. If the bookshelf door did exist and was removed, it is not at all clear when, by whom, and for what purpose.[9]

Moreover, there is another testimony which hopelessly complicates the information. Faurisson interviewed Miep and her husband Henk, who are supposed to have discovered the diary. According to them, the bookshelf door had been completed *before* the Franks arrived at the "hideout"![10] This is even though the diary states that it was created *after* the Frank family arrived at the "hideout". My guess is that Miep felt that it was unrealistic to say that the entrance was camouflaged by construction work after the Frank family came to live in hiding, and arranged the story in her own considerate way.

We cannot make out the truth of it. However, there is one clear physical fact. As we have already seen in the first chapter, placing the bookshelf door at the entrance to the Annex did not make the Annex a "hideout". At best, it could only hide the door itself leading to the third floor of the annex. As mentioned above, bookshelf door had no meaning, something that Otto agreed with in an interview by Professor Faurisson. Therefore, the most logical conclusion is that bookshelf door could not have been made, because such a thing would not make sense. If the entrance to the "hideout" had only been an ordinary door, Silberbauer

---

[9] This is highly suspicious, and makes one suspect, yet again, that the truth is something other than what is portrayed in the diary. It appears similar to other post-war Holocaust alterations, such as with the "gas chambers" at Dachau.
[10] Faurisson sec. 60.

would have remembered pushing the inward-opening door open. It can be inferred that his testimony that he "pushed open the furniture door" was influenced by this.

Did the Police Miss the Diary in Front of Them?

How was the diary left in the "hideout" and how was it recovered after the war? There is, in fact, a serious complication of information about this. Richard Harwood wrote in his book *Did Six Million Really Die?*:
"he returned to the Amsterdam house and 'found' his daughter's diary concealed in the rafters" (part 6).

To be precise, "rafter" refers to the pillars that make up the roof, so it is impossible to hide the diary there; Harwood must have been referring to the attic. Several acquaintances of my generation had the same perception. Seeing that this theory is still widely recognized, this may have been the official setting in the early post-war period, but there is no confirmation.

The theory that Otto found it in the attic is at least not the current official version. By 1958, at the latest, the theory was established that Miep and her colleagues went into the "hideout" the week after the Frank family was taken away, found the diary, retrieved it and handed it to Otto on his return to Holland after the war.

At the time of the above-mentioned questioning of Silberbauer, Otto himself was also questioned on 2 December 1963. However, he made a fatal mistake in his testimony in relation to this case:

> This man's name, I later learned, was Silberbauer. He ordered me in a curt, barrack-room tone of voice to show him where we kept our money and jewelry. I pointed out where they were. Then he picked up a briefcase in which my daughter Anne kept her papers, including her diary notes. He shook the briefcase out onto the floor and then put our jewelry and our money into it. (RCE, p. 22)

Firstly, according to this, Silberbauer, the German SS man, confiscated the Frank family's cash and jewelry, but what was the legal basis for this action?

As far as I know, the Nazis generally, and the SS in particular, were a very rule-abiding organization. SS men were held to the highest standards, both with respect to Germans and to other people, including even Jews. Many transgressions, such as theft of private property, were punishable by death. It is therefore highly questionable that the Silberbauer group as described in Otto's testimony was a gang of malicious, violent thieves who robbed people of their valuables at random.

Aside from this, there is one aspect of Otto's testimony that is extremely hard to believe. Silberbauer himself spread Anne's diary books and a large number of loose-leaf on the floor! And upon doing so, he paid no attention to them!

Needless to say, the task of the police is to maintain public order. The German police were trying to arrest political resistance groups and terrorists. Naturally, the reason for searching Otto's company and residence was to find any illegal activities of the people involved, such as links to resistance groups. A dated and written account of events in the building, such as a diary, should rightly have been the most important evidence. Moreover, Anne's diary was very mature in handwriting and content. Especially in the case of a diary written on loose-leaf, the text of which is bare, one would have known at a glance that it was a record of some kind. What did the police seize and what were they investigating if they missed these?

Moreover, there were eight police. Could it be that all eight of them were negligent and incompetent police who, like starving beasts, only wanted expensive goods? What's more, the police returned to the building three more times to continue their search, but the diary was never seized.

On the other hand, Silberbauer testified to journalists that he did not believe in the authenticity of the diary at all. He did not see anything of the kind in the building. He would not have known that Otto had testified that he himself had spread the diary on the floor. And, of course, the anonymous witnesses who cooperated with Faurisson did not testify about the diary. Otto also testified that Anne's work was kept in a bag.

Otto may have thought he had it all worked out, but this set-up led to a number of other glitches. Firstly, in the period before her arrest, Anne was supposed to have been busy editing her own work. If this is the case, it is impossible to do so without having all the manuscripts and diaries she had written up to that point close at hand. In other words, she couldn't leave her finished manuscript all tucked away in her bag. If this is correct, then Anne would have repeatedly put all her work in a bag after each day of writing and editing. This can seem like an extremely complicated procedure. However, it is not necessarily incomprehensible if we interpret it as the fact that she wanted to escape with the bag, which was more important than anything else, in case of emergency. In any case, there is no mention of the bag in the diary, even though it is an important matter.

And if this is correct, then all Anne's works fell around the place where Silberbauer was standing. According to Otto's testimony, "He shook the bag out on the floor", which means that if the paper was scattered on the floor, it was at most within the distance that it would be scattered from the height of an adult man's chest while it fell to the floor. However, according to Schnabel, Miep and Bep, who allegedly collected these diaries, testified as follows:

> It was terrible, when I went up there. Not a soul in the place. The rooms suddenly looked so big. Everything had been turned upside down and rummaged through. On the floor lay clothes, papers, letters and school notebooks. Anne's little wrapper hung from a hook on the wall. I took it with me. And among the papers on the floor lay a notebook with a checked red cover. ... I, too, saw the papers on the floor, and I said to Miep: 'Look, Miep, there is Anne's handwriting, too.' We sat down on the floor and leafed through all the papers. They were all Anne's, the notebooks and the colored duplicate paper from the office, too. We gathered them up and took them down with us. Downstairs, in the main office, we locked up all of it.

A few days later M. came into the office, M. who now had the keys to the building. He said to me: 'I found some more stuff upstairs.' What he gave me was more of Anne's papers... (pp. 190-191)

According to Miep, the items were scattered all over the floor, but common sense dictates that the police do not carry out such a rough search. Moreover, Schnabel himself wrote on another page that "the police acted with great quietness":

What happened in the house on the Prinsengracht on that fourth of August, 1944, was far less dramatic than it is now depicted on the stage. In reality the automobiles did not approach with howling sirens, did not stop with screaming brakes in front of the house. The bell was not rung. No rifle butt rapped against the door till it reverberated as it now reverberates in the theater every night somewhere in the world. The truth was, at first no one heard a sound. They were practiced, skillful, and quiet in such cases. (pp. 129-130)

Moreover, if the police were so persistent in their search, the question again arises as to why they did not seize a single copy of Anne's daily records. Were they only looking for valuables and money?

According to their testimony, the diaries were scattered all over the house, including on different floors (!), which clearly does not correspond to Otto's testimony. In particular, unlike the edited version, which is said to have been written on loose-leaf, the heavier "diary book" would have fallen straight down, i.e. in roughly the same place as other diary books. Therefore, Miep must have picked them up all together. Anyway, this is how the diary was recovered. In particular, not a single page of the edited version has been found to have been left out, which means that almost all of the pages have been found.

"Margot's Diary," and Other Missing Items

However, this causes other problems. This is because, according to the description in the diary, the following items, which should have existed, have not been recovered at all:

1) *The family tree made by Anne.* One of Anne's hobbies was to compile family trees of the royal families of various countries, which seems too academic a hobby for a girl of 14. On 20 May 44 she wrote about a "whole portfolio of family trees". This seems to have been a very important item for her, so she must have kept it in her bag every day and it must have fallen on the floor with her diaries.

2) *"Too long stories" by Anne.* As mentioned above, on 21 Apr 44 there is a reference to "too long stories" by Anne. For some reason, however, no such manuscript has ever been found.

3) *A reply to a letter received from Margot.* Anne carefully transcribed the text of Margot's letter on 22 Mar 44 etc. She also transcribes the text of her own letter to Margot. However, neither of these original letters has been found. In particular, the letter from Margot must have been kept in this bag.

4) *The (lost) second diary.* As mentioned above, there are a total of three diary versions in existence today. Theoretically, there should also have been a fourth, chronologically speaking, second diary book in the period 5 Dec 42 to 22 Dec 43. As the diary version is an essential document when writing the edited version, it is natural that it would have been placed in the bag with the other diaries. Why has this diary book been lost, when it would have fallen in almost the same place as the other diaries?

5) *Drafts of works.* As Faurisson points out, it is a very strange fact that the manuscript attributed to Anne contains very few corrections. However, it is impossible for any writer to produce a finished manu-

script without revision and editing. This is evident in the manuscripts full of corrections by historical writers. Thus, Anne's writing, which is as accomplished as that of a professional writer, can be interpreted as being entirely copied from drafts. In fact, on 9 May 44, it says, "I've finished my story of Ellen the fairy. I have copied it out on nice note paper." After all, no matter how genius Anne was, she couldn't write a polished, final text on first go. If so, there must have been a large number of drafts in existence at the time when she was in the middle of editing, which she kept in her bag at all times. However, not a single draft by Anne is known to exist.

6) In addition to these, I should like to point out that there is another object which should be found but is not, even if it was not kept in the bag in question. It is a *diary by Margot*.

On 14 Oct 42, it is stated that Margot also kept a diary:

> Margot and I got in the same bed together last evening, it was a frightful squash, but that was just the fun of it, she asked if she could read my diary sometime, I said yes at least bits of it, and then I asked if I could read hers... (A-version)

> *Gisteren avond lagen Margot en ik samen in mijn bed, het was onnoemelijk klein maar juist grappig, ze vroeg of ze soms mijn dagboek mocht lezen; ik zeg sommige stukken wel, en toen vroeg ik naar de hare dat mocht ik dan ook lezen...*

Why doesn't this other diary exist? Or even any trace of it? I would very much like to read Margot's diary, as she is said to have been a much more mature and honorable student than Anne.

The Shocking Truth! Did Anne Give Up Her Diary?

But the most absurd thing in the official story is not, in fact, this story of how diary was recovered by Miep and his friends. Rather, it is the reason why the diaries were eventually left on the floor of the "hideout". If you were to ask people who had no prior knowledge of Anne's diary, what would they say about it? Perhaps something like this:

> "The police suddenly raided Anne's 'hideout' and took them away in a flash, like kidnappers. As a result, Anne and the residents were left with no choice but to leave the diary in the 'hideout'…"

Perhaps it is something like this. In fact, I was one myself. Whatever the truth, I had a preconceived notion that this was the case, at least as an ostensible explanation. The now-forgotten explanation that the diary was hidden in the attic and only discovered after the war is essentially the same. But the truth was rightly astonishing.

Otto testified to Schnabel about the circumstances of their departure from the "hideout" as follows:

> They gave us more time than we needed. We all knew what we had to pack—the same belongings we had planned on taking in case of fire.
>
> Once Anne came to me and I said: 'No, don't take that, but you can take that along.' And she obeyed, for she was very quiet and composed, only just as dispirited as all the rest of us. Perhaps that was why she did not think to take along one of her notebooks, which lay scattered about on the floor. But perhaps, too, she had a premonition that all was lost now, everything, and so she walked back and forth and did not even glance at her diary. (pp. 139-140)

Do you understand? According to this testimony, it was Anne's and Otto's *intention* to leave the diary strewn on the floor when they left the "hideout"! Moreover, although they had "already decided" what they would take with them in case of emergency, they did not take the diary with them! Moreover, they did not entrust the diary to Miep and others.

That Otto and the others had been given time to pack is confirmed by the testimony of Kleiman: "It all took a long time" (p. 137). Therefore, according to Otto's testimony, the diary was ignored by the police, abandoned by Otto and Anne, left on the floor, then picked up by Miep and others, and returned to Otto again after the war.

What a dumb story!

However, in her entry of 11 Apr 44, Anne wrote "Not my diary; if my diary goes, I go with it!" in response to the statement "burn the diary". Wasn't her diary as important to Anne as her life? And, in fact, according to Otto, he had packed her writings in his bag so that he could take them out at any time in case of emergency. So why did Otto lose interest in taking it as soon as the contents were spread out on the floor? Why did Anne suddenly become so indifferent to diary? Otto does not say why he left his diary behind. However, he explains that Anne did not take the diary with her because "she had a premonition that all was lost now". But on the other hand, at the end of 11 Apr 44, she also writes,

> Be brave! Let us remain aware of our task and not grumble,
> a solution will come, God has never deserted our people.

Wasn't Anne Frank, a girl with an indomitable spirit, not supposed to despair so easily? Or is it that she wrote such brave things in writing, but when the time came, she was so upset that she lost her ability to make decisions? However, Otto also stated that "she was very quiet and composed".

In the end, why did Anne and Otto make the decision to not take diary with them? It is incomprehensible to me.

We should remember that the diary contained many details that she could not show to others, such as the love affair with Peter, menstruation, interest in sex, and the description of her own genitals. Anne, an adolescent girl, left the "hideout" with it *on the floor*. If we are to support the hypothesis that Anne's diary was written by Annelies, we must also accept the more important testimony of this most important person. Of course, I can't believe such a nonsense story.

Why Did Anne Get a Gorgeous Book, But Not a Diary?

In response to the previous analysis, it may be argued that the diary actually exists in physical form. In fact, the diary books themselves are extremely suspicious.

First of all, of the three existing diaries, the first one is a red and white checkered notebook that looks like something a girl would like. But the second and third notebooks are very plain and designed in such a way that a girl would never choose them. The reason for this seems to be that Anne had a hard time getting her notebook because she lived in a "hideout". As mentioned above, for the last diary, "Margot made it herself by tearing apart a chemistry notebook".

However, this interpretation doesn't hold up because even in the "hideout" it is explained that an incredible number of goods were obtained. On 13 Jun 44, Anne received a large number of birthday presents, just after Margot made the diary book. These include a five-volume art history book, a botany book, and a note book (*Schriften*)! It is actually written in the diary itself that there is no way she could not have gotten a notebook with a pretty design that a girl would like.

And there is a simpler and more serious contradiction in the first diary book. According to the order listed in the official version, the page with photos and letters from Otto starts right after the diary version 19 Jun 42, and continues for a long time. The date of Anne's comment on it is 28 Sep 42 five times. In other words, the date is suddenly skipped by three months. However, the date then reverted to 30 Jun 42, i.e., the continuation of the original date. There are somehow five September 28th's written on the page between June 19 and June 30. Even if the page was tacked on later, it is extremely strange that the date is reversed like this. There is only one reason for these strange occurrences: the sloppiness of the person who physically forged the diary.

Who Wrote the 'Handwriting of the Same Person'?

As we have seen, everything related to Anne's diary is full of falsehoods and deceptions: the content itself, the testimonies of those involved, the manipulation of information by the Dutch authorities, and every other element. If you still want to believe that this diary is written by Annelies, the last remaining evidence would be a handwriting analysis.

However, at least in the current situation, even this is not evidence at all. This is because the purpose of handwriting analysis is to determine whether multiple handwritings are that of the same person—nothing more and nothing less. Sample A and Sample B are compared, and then we inquire whether both were written by the same person. Who, precisely, that person is, is another matter entirely.

The handwriting that is attributed to Annelies has been authenticated as being that of "the same person." I am a novice in this field, but my personal impression is that this is correct. However, if it was written by the same person, whether that person is Annelies or someone else entirely, it is quite natural that the handwriting would be identified as that of the same person. After all, Annelies had conveniently died during the war, so there was no way to get her to write the letters for authentication.

The only thing that the official side submitted as evidence that the diary belonged to Annelies was the handwriting on an envelope and a postcard. However, from the standpoint of my original field of study, the Holocaust controversy, I can argue that it is easy to forge such materials. In fact, there is a lot of falsified evidence related to the Holocaust. As far as I know, there are about 20 of them, including official documents, diaries, letters, recording disks, drawings, and photographs. All of them are so clever that the average person would not notice that they are forgeries at all at first glance. The official side has committed a number of forgeries and cover-ups. It is an officially recognized fact that the bookshelf door has now been rebuilt.

Even the official version, which is considered to be the most detailed document at present, can be expected to contain a lot of partial information, concealment, and falsification. One obvious example is the entry of 20 February 1944. This used to exist in the published version, and still exists in the Definitive Edition of 2001. But it was completely removed from the RCE in 2003, probably because of criticism by Faurisson.

Therefore, we should be skeptical about the materials submitted by the official side for handwriting analysis as well. For example, the postcard in Figure 26 was submitted for handwriting analysis. The name on the front and the text on the back are in Otto's handwriting, but only the handwritten typeface in the upper left corner of the front (circled by the oval) was authenticated as being by Annelies. However, this is only an assertion of fact by the authorities. These words could be easily written later, even by a different person. If it is the same person who wrote the diary, then obviously, the handwriting will match.

Fig. 26 (official version, p. 138)

Figure 27 was submitted for appraisal as a letter by Annelies in an envelope, but "in an envelope" is also merely an assertion.

However, in August 1988, the first samples of Annelies' handwriting were found outside the official side. Figure 28 is an image of the two letters she sent to her pen pal in the U.S. and the enclosed postcard.

Unfortunately, the letters date from April 27 and 29, 1940, before the (alleged) start date of Anne's diary. However, since the earliest date in the standard handwriting by Anne submitted for handwriting analysis is 30 June 1941—see Figure 29—the time gap is only about one year. Compare this with Anne's handwriting in 1944 side by side.

Fig. 27 (official version, p. 134)

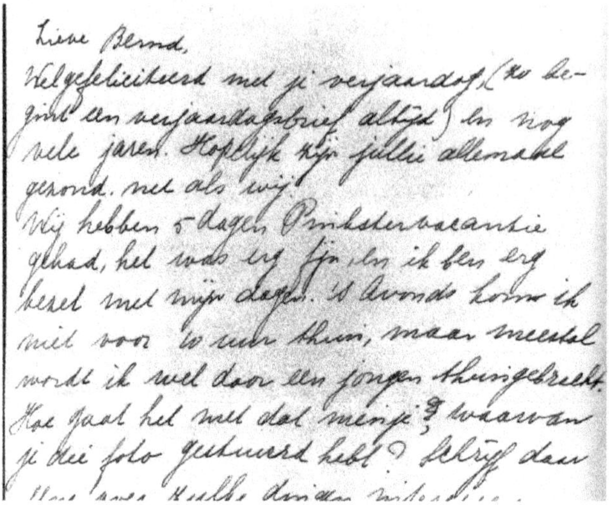

Lieve Bernd,
Welgefeliciteerd met je verjaardag! (zo be-
gint een verjaardagsbrief altijd) en nog
vele jaren. Hopelijk zijn jullie allemaal
gezond, net als wij.
Wij hebben 5 dagen Pinkstervacantie
gehad, het was erg fijn en ik ben erg
bezet met mijn dagen. 's Avonds kom ik
niet voor 10 uur thuis, maar meestal
wordt ik wel door een jongen thuisgebracht.
Hoe gaat het met dat meisje, waarvan
je die foto gestuurd hebt? Schrijf daar

Fig. 28 "Anne Frank's Handwriting Robert Faurisson"
New York Times, 22 July 1988, p. A1.

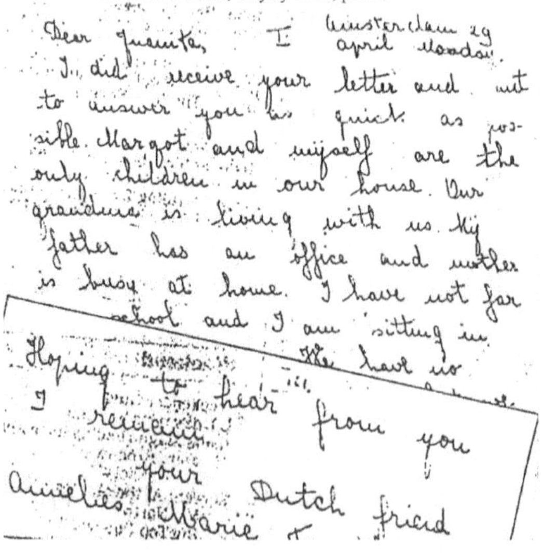

Dear Juanita, I Amsterdam 29 april Monday.
I did receive your letter and want
to answer you as quick as possible. Margot and myself are the
only children in our house. Our
grandma is living with us. My
father has an office and mother
is busy at home. I have not far
school and I am sitting in
We have no
Hoping to hear from you
I received
your Dutch friend
Annelies Marie

Fig. 29 standard handwriting by Anne 30/6/1941
(official version, p. 126)

23/3/1944 (official version, p. 577)

It should be noted that the dates given in the standard handwriting are also self-reported by the official side. There is no way to prove that it was really written on that date.

Even if we are laymen when it comes to handwriting analysis, it should be obvious: The handwriting found in the U.S. is unique, with an unusual slant to the left, while the standard handwriting by Anne is quite masterful, with a beautiful slant to the right. In addition to that, the two handwritings in Figure 29 should have been separated by three years of age, but there is almost no difference between them.

I am a layman when it comes to handwriting analysis, so I will refrain from making any further comments. I would like to leave it to the readers to make their own judgments. The Annelies letter in question, which was found in the U.S., has not yet been submitted for handwriting analysis, and probably never will be.

According to Faurisson's report, he seems to assume that the handwriting on diary is by Isa Cauvern, a woman who allegedly helped Otto with the publication of Anne's diary.[11] And he insists that the handwriting by Isa should be authenticated.

Strangely enough, this woman committed suicide just before the Dutch version was published. The connection between this suicide and the publication of Anne's diary is unknown.

---

[11] And wife of Albert Cauvern, as discussed in the Foreword.

CHAPTER 5

THE DIARY UNMASKED

Did Otto Write the Diary?

Now, it is time to explore the last mystery about Anne's diary. If the diary is not a wartime work by Annelies, as I have claimed, then there was someone who created it after the war. Who is it?

A common myth is that it was written by her father, Otto. Faurisson also thinks that there is no doubt that Otto was at least deeply involved in the creation of the diary. Unfortunately, there is no clear evidence to draw any conclusions about this. Therefore, anything I write after this is merely a psychological consideration and speculation based on various circumstantial evidence.

As a matter of fact, at a time when I myself had little interest in this issue, I had a vague impression that Otto may have authored the diary. This is simply because he is the closest to Annelies, and there is no other reason for this. However, as I took in the information related to Anne's diary this time, my thoughts changed. Of course, without Otto's help, the writing of diary would not have been possible. However, there must have been another main writer who took the initiative in writing the diary.

First of all, as a basic premise, fabricating and publishing a diary by a girl who died in a camp is a tremendously abnormal act. This requires more than just writing, but also the physical fabrication of a diary book. And it includes the need to devise a way to make it look as authentic as possible so that the fabrication is not discovered. This is not an idea that comes from a sane person. To do this requires very strong motivation. Furthermore, as already mentioned, the writing style in the diary is very advanced. There is a deep sense of culture, insight, and sometimes intense Jewishness included. It is difficult for a girl, or even an average adult, to write this. In other words, to produce Anne's diary, one must also have the ability to do so.

First, regarding motive, did Otto perhaps write the diary for money or fame? Was there any chance that such a book could be published at that time? What were the hopes for its commercial success? With some experience in the banking industry, Otto would have been basically a practitioner. He would have had no reason to think that he could pull off a major literary fraud. It is hard to imagine that he would choose a highly uncertain means of publishing to make money and gain prestige.

So, is the motivation for writing based on some ideological belief? However, Otto, by his own admission, had a weak Jewish identity and was rather a patriotic German citizen. Although of Jewish ancestry, he admitted to himself that he was of little religious faith. Nor is it said that he was strongly political. Therefore, it is unlikely that Otto wrote the diary based on ideology or faith.

Alternatively, the diary could be interpreted as a record of the life of a deceased daughter, even if it was fabricated, and motivated by some sort of warped desire for publicity or remembrance. However, this is also unnatural for reasons discussed below.

As for ability, this is even more decisive. As I said about Annelies, the vast and detailed writing of the diary is the work of a natural-born writer. Such a person should have left a large body of writing both before and after the diary. The fact is, however, that Otto's writings are unknown. It is possible to interpret that he did not publish any of his works after the war to prevent his fabrications from being discovered, but even before and during the war, no works by him existed. He enrolled at the University of Heidelberg, but dropped out after just one semester. There is no mention of any academic activity after that.

Thus, when we take the official information and the testimonies of those involved together, the character of Otto Frank clearly lacks both the motive and the ability to perform this insane act of producing a diary. There was, however, at least one person in Otto's vicinity who definitely possessed those qualities.

The Untold Confusion. And a Writer.

On 5 October 1955, a play based on Anne's diary had its premiere. It was a huge success in many countries and won the Pulitzer Prize that year. However, behind the scenes of this play, there was an intense and unknown internal conflict. Late the following year, one writer filed a lawsuit against the play's producers, Kermit Bloomgarden and Otto Frank.

This writer's name is Meyer Levin.

In fact, he also wrote the screenplay for the play. However, Levin's screenplay was rejected by a total of sixteen producers. This meant that Levin lost the right to market his scenario according to his contract, and Otto Frank asked Albert Hackett and his wife to write it for him. Levin disagreed and sought $200,000 in damages. The New York Supreme Court dismissed Levin's claim that Otto had breached the contract and committed fraud. However, the jury was left to decide on the other claim, that the Hacketts' scenario was an unauthorized plagiarism of Meyer's scenario. The jury returned a verdict in favor of Levin, "Otto and Bloomgarden must pay Levin $50,000 in damages," which was thrown out by the trial judge. Although Levin's version barely retained the right to perform the play only in Israel, it was in effect a total defeat for Levin. Levin continued to hold grudges against Otto and others involved in the play after the trial. The trial led to the misconception in some quarters that Otto had plagiarized portions of Levin's work to write the diary. However, as already mentioned, Levin's actual claim was that the Hacketts plagiarized parts of Levin's work to write the screenplay. Could the reason for this widespread misunderstanding be that Levin has been suspected as the true author in the forgery scandal since the diary was published?

Who is this Meyer Levin?

The following is a list of Levin's connections with the diary, extracted from the official version:

- November 20, 1950. Levin praised Anne's diary in the Jewish Council's journal.
- March 31, 1952. Otto appoints Levin as his copyright agent in the U.S.

- June 30, 1952. *National Jewish Post* published a review of the book by Levin. "A play or movie should be made based on this book."
- July 1952, at Levin's urging, producer Cheryl Crawford was approached to stage the play.
- September 1952, a radio program by Levin on the subject of the diary is broadcast.
- October 1952. Script by Levin completed. However, Crawford showed it to his friend Lillian Hellman and refused to perform it.

Looking at the timeline in this way, a simple question arises as to why Levin was appointed as the copyright agent in the U.S. in March 1952. At that point, the play he was working on did not even have a screenplay, let alone a decision to perform it. It was not until later that a radio program by Levin was realized. His novels had not achieved any commercial success, and he did not have any experience writing screenplays. Despite this, being appointed as a copyright agent is an unnaturally favorable treatment. How could such trust exist between Otto and Levin?

Where was Levin born? When, where, and what did he do?

The official version of the text states only that Levin is simply an "American journalist." Ordinary informational websites have almost nothing further on his background. A deeper search, though, uncovered an entry on www.encyclopedia.com, and more importantly, the book *Avengers and Defenders* (2008), by Walter Roth. This book describes the past lives of Jewish citizens from Chicago, and one chapter is devoted to Meyer Levin's writings during and after the war. Also enlightening is Levin's own book, *The Obsession* (1973). Together, these documents reveal a remarkable array of facts about the man. The following information was taken from the above sources.

A Passion Bordering on Madness

Levin was an American born in Chicago on 8 October 1905. He was a very well-educated man, having earned his doctorate from the University of Chicago in 1924. He was also such an accomplished writer that he received the National Jewish Book Award in 1966 and 1967. It should be noted that he immigrated to Palestine when he was a young man and lived in a kibbutz—a Jewish agricultural community—from 1928. Although he was an American born and raised in the U.S., he went all the way to Palestine to experience communal living with Jews. In fact, although Levin's nationality was American, he was of Jewish descent, having immigrated from Eastern Europe. In *The Obsession*, Levin stated that as a Zionist and socialist Jew, he fell victim to a Stalinist, anti-Semitic conspiracy within the United States (RCE, p. 82)

Let's trace Levin's career a bit further. He served as a war correspondent during the Spanish Civil War and moved to Hollywood after the outbreak of World War II. Quite interestingly, after working as a writer for defense projects, he worked for the Office of War Information, producing wartime propaganda films. He also went to England and worked in wartime propaganda with the Psychological Warfare Division in the United States (see Figure 31).

Fig. 31 Avengers and Defenders– Walter Roth. p. 91

Meyer Levin and Kibbutz Buchenwald Diary

In 1938, Chicago author Meyer Levin returned to the United States from his travels in Spain and Israel with his wife, the chemist, Mable E. Schamp, who gave birth on June 18, 1938 in suburban Glencoe to Levin's first son, Eli (also now known as Jo Batiste).

With the outbreak of World War II, Levin moved to Hollywood. Initially he worked as a writer on defense projects, then made films for the Office of War Information, and later enlisted in the Army, serving briefly as a propagandist in the Psychological Warfare Division, posted to England. There, in 1943, he met Tereska Torres, whom he had come to know briefly in Paris when she was a young girl and he was studying with her father, the artist Marek Szwarc. Tereska would later become his second wife and the mother of another son, Mikael.

After D-Day, Levin landed in France, and, as an American war correspondent, embarked on a journey through Europe, writing reports carried by many American newspapers and magazines. In his autobiography *In Search* (1950), Levin describes his journey from Paris to Prague, the Battle of the Bulge, and the liberation of the first concentration camps.

Using the same method he employed in writing *Citizens* (1940), the story of the 1937 Memorial Day Massacre in Chicago, he now

His early works were two semi-documentaries. One was the screen-play for the film "My Father's House," released in 1947. The film alleg-edly recounts the life of a 10-year-old Holocaust survivor named David Halevy, who was separated from his father in Nazi-occupied Krakow, Poland. His father had promised him that they would be reunited in Pal-estine. After the war ended, David went to Palestine to be reunited with his father. On the ship, he meets someone who lost his family in an ex-termination camp. After a long journey, David is informed that his par-ents were murdered in the Holocaust. Even from this rough outline, we see that this cannot be considered a semi-documentary. It is pure fiction—and an ideological propaganda film. Another of Levin's docu-dramas is "The Illegals," which also deals with illegal immigration to Palestine.

A further notable work by Levin is *Kibbutz Buchenwald.* Levin was present when the Buchenwald camp was liberated by U.S. troops on 11 April 1945. Among the former inmates, some Jews formed a commune (kibbutz) on a nearby farm and began to live there. Allegedly, a young couple living there wrote a Hebrew diary of their experiences, and Levin supposedly translated this into English, and then published it. If this sounds familiar, we won't be surprised.

Fortunately, I was able to obtain a copy of this book—see Figures 32 and 33. At first glance, one notices suspicious points that make one wonder if this diary is really authored by the people of the kibbutz. The first entry in this diary was in early June 1945 and the last entry was on 18 January 1946. In between, the dates are in neat succession without major interruptions. As for the alleged authors of the various entries, they were replaced in relay fashion by a string of names: Chayim Meir Gottlieb, Shlomek Lazarovitch, Avram Gottlieb, and so on, one after another, to different people. The total number of people involved amounts to ten. So, was this diary "relayed"? Or was each entry excerpt-ed from ten different diaries written over a seven-month period, so that the dates could be connected? How was this supposed to work?

Fig.32

Fig.33

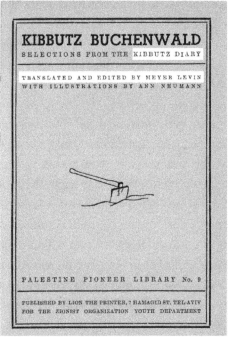

Moreover, all the writings are highly literary and political, and are not of a nature that could be called a diary in the general sense. I quote a few passages verbatim:

Rabbi Schechter said we must depend on our own selves. He spoke of the Jews of today who were like certain Jews who followed Moses but saw only difficulties and who said: No, we cannot secure the land of Israel. "Let us be like Joshua bin Nun," he declared, "like those who had the courage to rely on themselves, and who said 'Let us go up into the land'. Only then will we succeed."

We had a meeting with representatives of UNRRA and the Joint Distribution Committee, who came from Buchenwald to see us. Rabbi Schechter and Rabbi Marcus were also present. Mme Levy, of the Joint, told us how difficult it had been for this organization to secure permission to come to Germany to help the surviving Jews. But now that they were here, they would do everything in their power to assist us. ... (p. 16)

[T]hey claw at the earth with their fingers, but the earth is their own torn and bloody heart. As they reach deeper, the wound becomes bloodier. The strong can still endure, but the weaker ones break and fall into deep melancholy and endless sadness. Sometimes while the world sleeps peacefully, the sick souls of these people go out to meet each other; they dance, they sing happy tunes in doleful voices, they jest, and laugh at their own sickness. ...

We must inform you, beloved comrades, men and women, of the formation of a circle within a circle, for a new organization has been born into the kibbutz: the Society of the Falling Stars. Although we have long known that this is a community of lunatics, there was previously no clear organization and no programme for this element. Now, both have been provided. Last Saturday afternoon, eleven members of the kibbutz suddenly had a revelation.

Why, it came upon us, why should we continue to live like
ordinary human beings? Why try to imitate the life of normal people who never went through such a devil's dance as
ours? It is unnatural, it is even deceptive for us to attempt to
approach human problems with earnestness and modesty; it
is wrong for us to tie ourselves to people, earth, and time.
No! We scorn such an attitude. For in the ghetto and in
prison we secured a new outlook upon life. ... (p. 40)

In a secret spot deep in the woods, in a place where
normal, empty folk never penetrate, we eleven stars came
together, and in an historic moment we created our society
of the falling stars. Chavera S. was unanimously chosen as
chief falling star. She will show us the way. She will show
us where to fall. And in beginning this new life between
heaven and earth, we have taken new names upon ourselves. The girls are Venus, Aphrodite, Diana, Minerva,
and the boys are Apollo, Mars, Zeus, Neptune, Saturn,
Mercury, and Pluto. With these new names we enter our
new life. ... (p. 41)

Were there so many people in the kibbutz with such a talent for writing?
No matter how one interprets it, it is suspicious. Considering Levin's career as a wartime propagandist, this is clearly a book written in diary form
by Levin himself, based on interviews with people living on the kibbutz.

If we examine Levin's career, the following portrait emerges: An
extremely thoughtful and talented creator. A man with a strong fighting
spirit. A hardcore Jew who moved all the way from the U.S. to Palestine
to experience living together with Jews. Hard-line Zionist. A professional
who mixes false information with real information, produces and dissem-
inates propaganda films and books under the guise of documentaries, and
directs public opinion. As mentioned above, the script by Levin was rejected by producers at every turn. It is said that the reason was that his
style was "too Jewish."

Once again, comparing Otto Frank's character to Levin's, Otto is too
ordinary to produce the Diary of Anne Frank project. On the contrary, it is

someone like Levin, with a kind of insane passion and talent, who is the right person to do it. For Levin, immediately after the war, contributing to the realization of the State of Israel was the very purpose of life. No one was more intensely motivated than he was to bring the suffering and trage-dy of the Jews to the world, in order to boost the Zionist movement; if he could do so via a Jewish girl and her diary, all the better. His works "My Father's House", *Kibbutz Buchenwald*, "The Illegals" and "Anne's dia-ry" are completely on the same line in terms of his creative motivation.

In addition to these semi-documentaries, his work on propaganda films and wartime propaganda are also of the same nature in that they are falsehoods cleverly mixed with truths to give the appearance of being non-fiction. And it is exactly the same quality with the writing of Anne's diary. Again, he undoubtedly had the ability and experience to write such a diary. In particular, the idea of physically forging a diary, while crazy in common sense, would have been quite natural to Levin, who was a member of the psychological warfare division of the U.S. Army.

So far, this is entirely plausible. However, that does not mean that Levin was actually involved in the creation of Anne's diary, which is logically another matter.

What if it was Otto who came up with the idea of publishing the dia-ry and Levin was not involved in the project? Let's say it was mere coin-cidence that Levin's creative work and Anne's diary had the same char-acter in terms of the effect they had on society. The first problem with this is that Otto has no experience in writing. Otto will then need to find a ghostwriter to write the manuscript. That probably means Jewish talent, which means that Otto has to find another uncommon talent equal to Levin. Of course, there is no indisputable evidence that Levin produced diary. However:

1) From a statistical standpoint, it is unlikely that there is more than one person in Otto's vicinity who has the special qualities that would combine the motivation and ability to produce Anne's diary
2) One such person, Levin, undoubtedly existed.

3) In March 1952, when Levin had ostensibly made no achievements on Anne's diary, he was appointed by Otto as a copyright agent in the United States for some reason.

The logical conclusion to be drawn from this circumstantial evidence is that Levin is the author of the diary. At the very least, he is the most likely candidate.

If there are any factors that conflict with this hypothesis, one is the timing of the writing. The last entry of *Kibbutz Buchenwald* was on 18 January 1946, as mentioned above, and the movie "My Father's House" was released in 1947. And since Anne's diary was also published in 1947, the production periods seem to overlap too much. However, *Kibbutz* is only a thin book of 120 pages at most. And Anne's diary is only one volume at most.

As a comparison, let us take this book as an example. It was mid-January 2020 when I was asked to write this book. I then began researching and writing for the book, in addition to my day job. However, even I was able to finish the work two months later, in mid-March. Of course, it is clear that work efficiency is considerably higher today, where editing can be done on a computer, than right after the war when it was handwritten. However, a creator as talented and passionate as Levin would have had plenty of time to write the original draft of Anne's diary during 1946. In fact, according to the official version, he completed the radio drama and play scripts in just a few months each.

Another problematic issue is language. Looking at Levin's background, it does not appear that he was fluent in Dutch. If he were to write Anne's diary, it is more likely that the language would have been English. Otto, however, understood English and Dutch. It is also possible, if there was another translation staff, that the Dutch version was produced from Levin's English manuscript. As mentioned above, oddly enough, the German version was almost a different text that could not have been translated from the Dutch version.

This mystery is solved if we interpret it as the result of the production of Dutch and German versions respectively from an English original. On the contrary, we have physical facts that are consistent with this hypothesis. Levin is a U.S. citizen, but as of April 1945, he was in Germany covering the Buchenwald camp. In 1948, he is said to have been living in France. In other words, he was in Europe when Anne's diary was produced, and was in close physical proximity to Otto, at just the right time to produce such a diary.

More Abysses: The Origin of a Legend

If Levin was the author of the diary, could it have been as a result of the Anne's Diary Project being *conceived by Otto*, and then Levin being later named as the author by Otto?

This is unnatural for the same reason as the Otto authorship hypothesis. Rather, it is more natural to assume that there was first a project conceived outside of Otto, and that the planner discovered Otto. When I first began writing this book, I had the unfounded belief that the publication of the diary by Otto for monetary purposes was first, and that his writings were consequently used to promote the Holocaust and the Zionist movement. However, that assumption changed when I learned about Levin's background. Perhaps this diary was a propaganda and information operation from the beginning. In other words, the existence of Annelies Frank was not a prerequisite for the project to publish the diary. Rather, the initial intent was to publish a book by a Holocaust victim, and Annelies was chosen as its author. This assumption answers the question, Why is Anne the (nominal) author?

Recall the testimony of Hanneli ('Lies'), who was a friend of Annelies:

> Anne and I were very close friends, you must understand that, and yet no one suspected that she could write. With Margot it would have been different. We thought Margot terribly talented and capable of anything. But Anne, you see, was just my friend...

So, why Annelies? To add credibility to the diary, a better-qualified person would have been the undisputed honor student Margot. So why not

Margot? Consider a photograph of the two sisters, viewed under the interpretation that the diary was propaganda—see Figure 35. Why Annelies? Was she prettier than Margot? Perhaps. But one thing for sure: Anne was younger—by over three years. When Anne was 13 and 14, Margot was 16 and 17. Margot was a young lady, but Anne was "just a girl." And brilliant writing coming from "a girl" is more impressive than from a young lady. We can imagine that these were the factors under consideration.

Why Annelies only? Otto seems to have been equally affectionate toward Margot. Why did he not publish the diaries of both daughters? In this respect, too, it would be unnatural to assume that the project was conceived by Otto.

Fig. 35 "All about Anne Frank" (poplar, p. 17)

アンネ12歳
ユダヤ人学校にて

マルゴー15歳
ユダヤ人学校にて

So how, exactly, would Levin have initiated this project? We can only speculate, but it seems clear that he was well-connected in the European Jewish community. Perhaps he used that network to learn about the Anne Frank story? Or perhaps some higher-ups in the network conceived the plan, and enlisted Levin to execute it? As of today, we simply do not know.

*****

Curiously, Anne's diary was praised by three prominent people even before its publication. This contributed greatly to making the difficult publication a reality. All three are of Jewish descent, including historian Jan Romain. The play's producer, Kermit Bloomgarden, is also Jewish, as are the Cauverns, who assisted Otto in publishing the first Dutch version.

As noted above, Levin lost the court case against Otto, but afterward Levin proposed that a committee representing the Jewish community be established to formulate a compromise plan. As a result, a committee was organized by Joachim Prinz and two others, and on 26 October 1959, a settlement was reached that was, alas, extremely disappointing to Levin.

Why a committee by the Jewish community? As a Japanese man, it is extremely difficult for me to understand. Couldn't the dispute between Levin and Otto be handled purely as a legal matter? Was their dispute a matter that could only be mediated by the Jewish Committee?

And finally, some interesting information about "My Father's House," for which Levin wrote the script. Apparently the funding for this film came from among Levin's vast Jewish connections: "The budget was provided mainly from wealthy Jewish residents of Palestine and [Jewish-]Americans, and the remainder from Zionist institutions".[1]

It is my current conclusion that the source of Anne's Diary Project is likely to be these people.

---

[1] Quoting from Wikipedia, "My Father's House," citing the Israeli journal *Davar* (5 Nov 1947).

AFTERWORD: ANNELIES NEXT TO YOU

Figure 36 is the text of a Christmas card sent by an Auschwitz inmate on Christmas Day 1943:

Fig. 36 HEALTHCARE IN AUSCHWITZ Carlo Mattogno p. 236

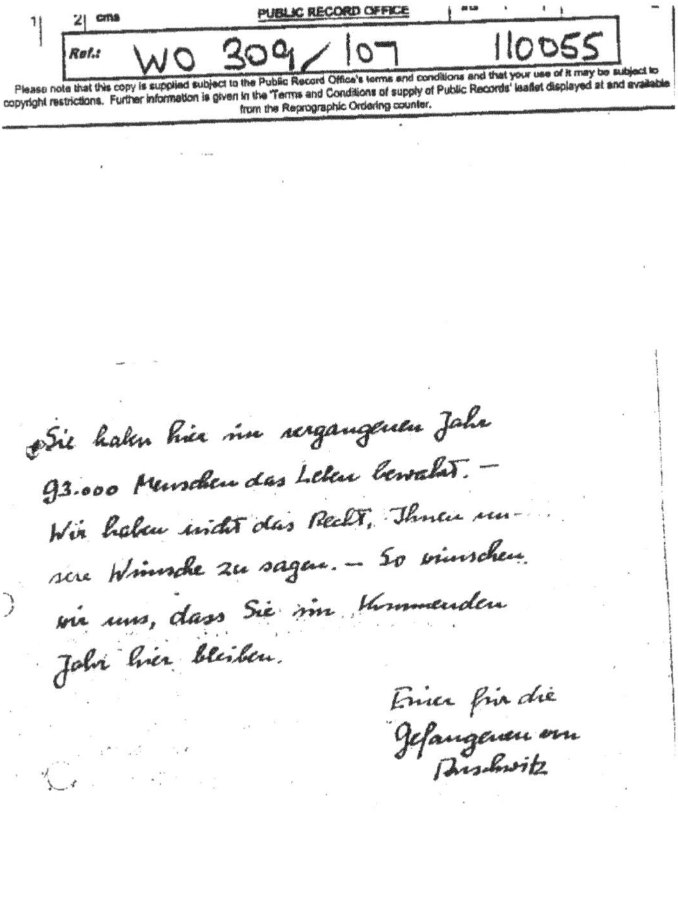

PUBLIC RECORD OFFICE

Ref.: WO 309/107 110055

Please note that this copy is supplied subject to the Public Record Office's terms and conditions and that your use of it may be subject to copyright restrictions. Further information is given in the 'Terms and Conditions of supply of Public Records' leaflet displayed at and available from the Reprographic Ordering counter.

Sie haben hier im vergangenen Jahr
93.000 Menschen das Leben bewahrt. –
Wir haben nicht das Recht, Ihnen un-
sere Wünsche zu sagen. – So wünschen
wir uns, dass Sie im kommenden
Jahr hier bleiben.

Einer für die
Gefangenen von
Auschwitz

It reads:

> In the past year you have saved the lives of 93,000 people.
> We do not have any right to express our wishes to you. –
> So, we wish to ourselves that you will remain here in the
> coming year.
>
> One, for the prisoners of Auschwitz

The recipient was Eduard Wirths, the SS chief physician at the Auschwitz camp from September 1942 until the camp closed in early 1945. He
was a devout Christian and a man of great integrity who devoted himself
to the sanitation of the camp and the treatment of the inmates. Among the
documents he left behind is the following interesting letter.

> For the damaged roofs of kindergarten blocks 29 and 31 in
> the Gypsy Camp I request 100 rolls of roofing felt (very
> urgent.)[1]

His gentle personality is evident in the way he adds "urgent" to his letter
to repair the roof of the children's playground. But he was not the only
exceptionally virtuous person who wanted to reduce the number of
deaths in the camps. As mentioned earlier, it was of paramount importance for the Nazis not to reduce the workforce in the camps, so they
rather thoroughly developed the living conditions in Auschwitz. Dr.
Wirths fulfilled his duties faithfully.

So why did Annelies die?

That Anne did not die in Auschwitz is basic knowledge that can be
found in any book related to her. She was transferred to the Bergen-
Belsen camp in Germany, where she died of illness a few months later.
In fact, the situation that led to piles of corpses in the camps occurred in
Germany in those camps that were not supposed to be extermination

---

[1] *The Rudolf Report*, 5.2.3.5 (Taken from a letter of 23 March 1944 to the Central Construction Office in Auschwitz, *Tsentr Chranenija Istoriko-
dokumental'nich Kollektsii* 502-1-332-175.)

camps. The reason for this is that the infrastructure, transportation net-work, and medical system were destroyed by indiscriminate attacks by the Allied forces. Ironically, it was *Allied actions*, not German actions, that led to piles of corpses at the camps.

In September and October 1944, Auschwitz was still dealing with a large influx of Hungarian Jews that arrived in June and July. The over-crowding, combined with Allied bombing, led to a health crisis in that camp, which makes it likely that Otto's wife Edith died of illness, not "gassing." But the worst situation was at Bergen-Belsen. Bombings completely disrupted the camp procedures, leading to grave typhus out-breaks and accumulation of corpses. Thus, Annelies and Margot were sent to the worst camp at the worst possible time.

But some readers may ask the question: "Wasn't there a gas chamber massacre at Auschwitz?" Correctly, that is the biggest point of contention. It is a little-known fact that in the current official Holocaust literature, as of October 1944, when Anne was transferred there, Auschwitz was the *only* place that was considered an extermination camp. All the other places that were supposed to be extermination camps—Treblinka, Belzec, So-bibor, and so on—had long been closed due to the Soviet invasion.[2]

If so, this makes for a very strange story. If the official version of the Holocaust is correct, then the Nazis were trying to *exterminate the Jews*. However, the Nazis did not change other camps to extermination camps, even though the number of extermination camps was decreasing rapidly. They then transferred Annelies *away from* Auschwitz, which was supposed to have gas chambers, to a camp (Bergen-Belsen) *without* gas chambers. Did the Nazis really intend to kill all the Jews? Where and how were they planning to kill Annelies? This is the greatest paradox in Anne's diary. Anne is perceived as a representative of Holocaust victims, but rather, ironically, the fate of Annelies Marie Frank is the most obvi-ous fact that *disproves* the Holocaust.

*****

---

[2] For the full story of what really happened at the German camps, see Thomas Dalton, *Debating the Holocaust: A New Look at Both Sides* (4th ed., 2020).

Returning to Dr. Wirths, after the war he was arrested by the Allied Forces as a criminal. He was considered a demon who was complicit in the genocide of the Jewish people. He was then driven to suicide. He was responsible for defending Annelies' life, but the propaganda that is damaging his dignity ironically includes The Diary of Anne Frank.

After the war, the reality of Nazism was thoroughly distorted. As many revisionists have shown in detailed studies, the Nazis sought to emigrate Jews voluntarily or forcibly, but no evidence of any attempted extermination exists. It is my hope that many people will be able to stand at a starting point where we can have a sober discussion about this Jewish emigration plan. However, this is made totally impossible by the flood of information manipulation or 'disinformation.' Without a doubt, Anne Frank is one of the strongest weapons in promoting this brainwashing. Therefore, this Anne's diary controversy is theoretically separate from the Holocaust controversy, but they are adjacent to each other across a very thin wall.

It is not only Germans who have been undermined by Anne's diary. The biggest victim is, of course, the soul of Annelies. Creating such a diary is an impermissible act, even if one reserves judgment on whether it was done with conviction for the sake of political propaganda. The reason I have gone on at length in my explanation of the Anne Matrix (see chapter two), knowing that it would be redundant, is to denounce the treatment meted out to her by those who produced the diary. These people created, cut and pasted, separated, pieced together, moved, changed, added to, or removed from the life of a young girl who had met a terrible and untimely end. They trumpeted political words, ideological words, and humanistic philosophies as her words as much as they wanted to. They added and deleted as they pleased: harsh criticism of the mother, invective against Mrs. van Pels, romantic feelings toward Peter, and even a description of the shape of her genitalia. Moreover—and this is the most important point—these were all done after Annelies' death, without her consent. What greater sacrilege could there be against the soul of the deceased?

If you want to get even slightly closer to the truth about Annelies before she died, forget any of her supposedly diary. Not a single word in it contains *her* truth. It is merely a prison for Annelies' soul, covered by a thick wall of falsehood in the name of a legend. Barely anything can be said to convey her true image except photographs and, perhaps, a letter she sent to a pen pal in the United States. All other textual information, even the testimonies of friends and relations, is too biased and too fraudulent to be believed.

Rather, I urge you to look at the very ordinary girls around you. Perhaps those children are Annelies. At the very least, I can believe that the girls next to you, just as they are, are much more like the real Annelies than the eternal fictional Anne Frank, playing out a legendary tale of deception.

*****

In publishing this English edition, I would like to offer my sincere thanks to several people. First, Yuji Sawaguchi, the planner of the Japanese edition. He not only provided me with a number of materials, but also some important perspectives.

And to both Dr. Dalton, who suggested publishing the English version, and Mr. Karl Haemers, who kindly agreed to edit it. They have brushed up on the original, made the structure more effective, and changed the text into something more dynamic, sometimes with wry humor.

Nevertheless, this book is a misfortune to this world for its very existence. The Diary of Anne Frank is a book that should never have existed in this world. If all people everywhere could share this same understanding, this book would not need to exist.

At the same time, in this sense, the publication of this book was an absolutely necessary task. As a revisionist and by profession, my main vocation is to be a "teacher". My mission is to disseminate the results of foreign researchers to the Japanese people. However, each revisionist is working on a different mission. As for this "diary," it happened to have been neglected and, although it was completely unexpected, I decided to take on the task myself. Perhaps the writing of this book will be the most important act I have performed in my lifetime.

Unfortunately, the life of the Anne Frank legend will be longer than mine. This will be a long battle. But as long as the life of that blasphemous book lasts, the mission of this book will not disappear. You who are reading this book and this Afterword may be living far into the future, long after I have left this world. As such, I would like to extend my heartfelt thanks and modest wishes to all those who have had the privilege of acquiring this book.

Please, build a better future.

Please know the facts.

And revision the world as you see it.

POSTSCRIPT:
RE-REBUTTING THE ANNE FRANK HOUSE

Karl Haemers

The Anne Frank House describes itself as

> established on 3 May 1957 in cooperation with Otto Frank,
> Anne Frank's father. We are an independent non-profit or-
> ganisation that runs a museum in the house where Anne
> Frank went into hiding and we try to increase awareness of
> Anne's life story all over the world.[1]

As such, the Anne Frank House (AFH) takes responsibility for respond-
ing to "deniers" (quotation marks in original). It also calls those who
question the authenticity of the diary "right-wing extremists," "deluded
eccentrics," "new and old Nazis," "holocaust deniers" (of course), and
other dismissive derogatory terms.[2]

Let us examine whether this dismissal and derogation by AFH of
other views on the authenticity of the Anne Frank diaries is valid. And let
us remember why it is important. AFH says: "The diary of Anne Frank is
an important document of the Holocaust, and since the Second World
War Anne Frank has become the most well-known symbol of the persecution of the Jews." This ascribes paramount significance to the diaries
for the entire Holocaust story, and so determining their authenticity becomes paramount as well.

To begin with, AFH says:

---

[1] "About Us," Anne Frank House https://www.annefrank.org/en/about-us.
[2] "The Authenticity of the diary of Anne Frank," Anne Frank House
https://www.annefrank.org/en/anne-frank/go-in-depth/authenticity-diary-
anne-frank.

People who have claimed, or still claim, that the diary is not genuine have a political agenda. They often also say or write that the Holocaust never happened. Or they try to prove that there were no gas chambers at Auschwitz, and that the figure of six million Jews murdered during the Second World War is an exaggeration.[3]

This book does not claim those things. In fact, Suzuki establishes a clear distinction between Holocaust revision and diary revision, while acknowledging affiliations. Other books and analyses of the diaries make no mention of such claims, such as some of the works of Robert Faurisson. He has indeed questioned the Holocaust story elsewhere, but his works devoted to the Anne Frank diary focus on it exclusively, and should be taken at face value. Still other Holocaust revisionists such as David Irving and Arthur Butz make only brief and passing references to the diary.[4]

The AFH claims:

People and organisations that deny or trivialise the Holocaust are attempting to exonerate and rehabilitate the National Socialist system. Or, by spreading doubts on the fate of the Jews during the Second World War, they try to undermine the state of Israel's right to exist.[5]

How AFH purports to know the motivations of those who question the authenticity of the diaries is not explained. Certainly this book nowhere seeks to establish a 4th Reich, nor eradicate the state of Israel. In the Introduction, we examined other works exploring the authenticity of the

---

[3] Ibid.

[4] Noted revisionist Germar Rudolf has stated, "Anne Frank did write herself that she intended to publish her writings as a novel. Hence, even those pieces that she herself wrote are to be understood as a novel…but not as a truthful diary. … It is dishonest to claim something is true if it is merely a novel" (*Lectures on the Holocaust*, 2005, p. 430).

[5] Ibid.

diaries, and found that they, too, do not attempt to assert either of these claims. None of the main revisionist authors examining the diaries have claimed they want to resurrect National Socialism. The main objective of this book is to establish historical accuracy and validity, and to redress falsehood where warranted. What other people and organizations do with such knowledge is their own affair.

By contrast, is it not likely that AFH has revealed its own objectives by ascribing motives to others which they do not have? Accusing others of such wild motives most likely means that AFH's motives are political and not historical: to preserve the Holocaust narrative against any revisionist efforts, to suppress knowledge of legitimate political positions (National Socialism and fascism generally), and to justify the existence of the nation of Israel. To paraphrase the Bard: Methinks AFH doth protest too much—imagining attacks against it and the diaries that do not exist. It is true that establishing the diaries as forgeries or fraud would undermine these objectives of AFH, and of many other powerful Jewish people and organizations, though that is not necessarily the goal of revisionists.

AFH continues:

> In Europe and North America, the distribution of material
> in which the authenticity of the diary of Anne Frank is at-
> tacked – and often that the Holocaust is denied – is fortu-
> nately only the work of a few people.[6]

The number of people who have distributed material questioning the diaries may be relatively few, but their number has been suppressed by the harsh consequences that can afflict them. Robert Faurisson was violently attacked by a Jewish mob, and other authors have faced persecution, ostracism, impoverishment, prison, defamation, and marginalization. This tends to unjustly reduce the number of authors and distributers. More importantly, it is not the quantity but quality of the presentation that matters, and that is what we should examine. In some sense, the more widely

---

[6] Ibid.

and stridently some historical story is promoted, the less likely it is to be true. The more restricted and suppressed a counter-story is omitted, the more likely it is to be true. Scope and reach do not matter for validity, only quality.

AFH also states:

> There are no serious scientists who doubt the fact that the Holocaust took place or that the diary of Anne Frank really was written by her.[7]

Our focus is the diaries, and the AFH itself states that a scientific investigation was conducted by Netherlands Forensic Institute in the early 1980s, by handwriting experts in Germany in 1959, and by the Federal Criminal Police Office in Germany also in 1980.

AFH refers to a summary of the Netherlands Forensic Institute report, not the report itself, when it claims

> The report of the Netherlands Forensic Institute has convincingly demonstrated that both versions of the diary of Anne Frank were written by her in the years 1942 to 1944. The allegations that the diary was the work of someone else...are thus conclusively refuted.[8]

The German handwriting experts in 1959 did not conclude that all the original writings in the diary as well as subsequent corrections and notations were written in Anne's handwriting, as AFH claims, but that simply they were all written *by the same person*. That person may or may not have been Anne.

The AFH claims the Federal Criminal Police Office in Wiesbaden Germany in 1980 concluded that the paper and ink used to make the diary were in use before 1950. The diaries were supposedly written between

---

[7] Ibid.

[8] Ibid. I have been unable to find a copy or file of the original report, and am awaiting response to an inquiry I have made to NFI.

1942 and 1944. This leaves a six-to-eight-year gap of possibility, at a time when post-war science and technology was producing new forms of paper and ink. If 1950 is the oldest date the investigation can identify for the paper and ink, then it may just as well have shown that the diary was written after 1944 as during or before. AFH is full of such vague and suggestive statements.

As another instance, AFH dismisses the interview Robert Faurisson conducted with Otto Frank in person, with Otto's second wife 'Fritzi' in attendance.[9] The only dismissal AFH offers is the following: "[A]ccording to Fritzi Frank, when he (Faurisson) examined the diary he said: 'It'll be very difficult to prove that the diary is a forgery'."[10] In a kind of hypnotic suggestion, AFH must intend this statement of Faurisson to mean that he thought the validity of the diary was solid, and thus hard to prove as a forgery. It is far more likely that Faurisson, if in fact he made such a statement, was referring to the many obstacles to questioning the diary that he encountered, including hostile witnesses, lawsuits, firing from his job as a professor, and even physical assault. They certainly made it difficult to prove that the diary was a forgery!

The Mysterious Five Pages

In another strange plot twist, five missing pages of the diary apparently surfaced in 1998. They were presented by a man named Cor Suyk (full name Cornelius Suijk) who AFH says was "a former employee" of AFH.[11] Others say Suiyk was a former Director of AFH.[12] Suiyk claims Otto Frank gave him the five pages for "safe keeping," and that "in all probability" (more vague language), Otto did not want them published until after his second wife died (in 1998) because they contained "Anne's rather hurtful observations about his first wife, who died in Auschwitz, and their marriage." The probability that this is the reason the five pages

---

[9] We recall that his first wife (and Anne's mother) Edith, died in Auschwitz in late 1944.

[10] Ibid.

[11] Ibid.

[12] Life Stories, Cornelius Suijk, interview by Lisa Chait (www.lifestories.co.za).

were withheld from publication declines when we notice that plenty of accounts in the Diary already are critical of Otto's first wife and first marriage.

Suiyk engaged in a prolonged, but successful, legal battle to ensure he owned the copyright to the pages. When this was completed, he then sold the pages to "the Dutch nation," held by the Netherlands State Institute for War Documentation (NIOD). Here we see another "generous philanthropist" concerned primarily with the memory of a suffering Jewish girl at the hands of evil "Nazis," profiteering from the sale of her alleged writings. AFH does not disclose the amount Suiyk received, but another source does—$750,000.

Suijk gave an interview in 2010 at the age of 86 to Life Stories ("preserving memories forever") founder Lisa Chait.[13] As with so many diary promoters, Suijk makes the most absurd and foolish statements as he tells the story of how Meip went to the annex to find the diaries. He says the German police had raided the place and locked it up, but that Meip had "spare keys." Are we to believe the Germans raided the Frank "hideout," apprehended the inhabitants, stole their loot, then locked the "hideout" up using the same locks and keys the inhabitants used? This is not standard police procedure, especially among efficient German police. Crime scenes are always promptly and thoroughly secured, with German-owned locks.

Next Suijk claims that Meip hid the diary documents in her office desk drawer, but did not lock it because the Germans would only look in locked drawers, not open drawers. He says, "That is the kind of intelligence Meip had." I confess, I laughed aloud when I read this. Is it truly 'intelligent' to hide documents that (Suijk claims) could get a person killed, in an *unlocked* desk drawer? Because the German police would only look in *locked* drawers? Rather, a reasonably intelligent person would say this is, in fact, stupidity. That, or an outright lie.

One reason Suijk gives that Otto did not want the five pages to be published is because they contained Anne's observation that Otto did not really love his first wife, Anne's mother Edith. This contradicts AFH,

---

[13] Ibid.

which says Anne made "hurtful observations" about Edith. Suijk says Anne's observations in the five missing pages are about Otto. In those pages, Anne apparently says that Otto only kissed his first wife in the same way he kissed his children, lacking the proper passion with which a husband should kiss his wife, "if you are in love." Suijk calls this a "very intelligent remark." Here again we see Anne the relationship expert as a young teen, critiquing her parent's displays of affection—or lack of them.

Suijk claims Otto received 5,000 letters from young girls asking his advice about their parents, because "they knew Otto was a wonderful father." Otto did not want to hurt their feelings or betray their confidence by publishing the five pages, because they would show that he was not, in fact, a wonderful husband. As we've seen, plenty that was already in the diary showed Otto was not a wonderful husband, so what special reason would he have for withholding the five pages? He couldn't let down those 5,000 girls by telling Anne's truth, now could he?

Fine, except that—it was okay with Otto after he and his second wife were dead. Why? Did he not care about his and his first wife's posterity? Was their reputation unimportant to him after they had died? Would it not look duplicitous and deceitful of him when the world found out he had been withholding some content of the Diary? Suijk presents this as something noble Otto did, but it could just as readily be seen as something ignoble and contemptible. Suijk claims that it was due to "integrity" that Otto did not want to withhold anything about the diary from the public, but we could equally claim it was deceit to withhold them for as long as he did.

Suijk discloses that after the legal battles and he was declared owner of the pages, he sold them to the Dutch government for $750,000, or $150,000 per page. He claims he gave the money to an "educational fund" in the US.

Suijk has still another reason Otto withheld the pages, and Otto's first marriage appears more debased and perverted because of it. The five pages supposedly say that Otto told Anne that he never forgot his first love, whom he wanted to marry but could not because Otto's father, a banker, lost all his money. Thus the parents of Otto's first love would not let her marry him. What kind of father would tell his early teen or younger daughter such a thing? Suijk tells us a "wonderful" father. It could be considered abuse for a father to confide to his young daughter that he really loved a woman other than her mother, his wife.

Also, presuming that Otto's first love was also Jewish, this story shows how crassly materialistic and money-obsessed Jews are, since her parents blocked true love merely because Otto's father went bankrupt. Presumably Otto and Anne readily accept this reason, as they are Jews with the same materialistic money-obsessed values.

Otto withheld this content of the Diary because he "wanted to protect himself and his (second) wife" from aggressive journalists, Suijk claims. Earlier, Suijk said Otto withheld the pages because he did not want to disappoint all the girls who wrote to him, believing him to be a "wonderful" father. Suijk thus gives conflicting motives.

The Life Stories website where Suijk's interview is displayed gives a link to the five pages themselves, but that shows a "403 Forbidden" message. Forbidden?! Why are we forbidden to see the five pages themselves? Nevertheless, I found them on the Anne Frank Forum website.[14] Here we see once again the unlikelihood that a teenage girl could write such adult, insightful material. Here is one extended, relevant section:

> I seem to be in a period of reflection at the moment, so I also started thinking of Father and Mother's marriage. It has always been presented to me as an ideal marriage. Never a quarrel, no angry faces, perfect harmony, etc., etc. I know a few things about Father's past, and what I don't know, I've made up; I have the impression that Father married Mother because he felt she would be a suitable wife. I have to admit that I admire Mother for the way she assumed the role of his wife and has never, as far as I know, complained or been jealous. It can't be easy for a loving wife to know she'll never be first in her husband's affections, and Mother did know that. Father certainly admired Mother's attitude

---

[14] Anne Frank Forum, February 21, 2006;
www.tapatalk.com/groups/annefrankfr/the-5-missing-pages-t59.html

and thought she had a good character. Why marry anyone else? His ideals had been shattered and he was no longer young.

What kind of marriage has it turned out to be? No quarrels or differences of opinion—but certainly not an ideal marriage. Father respects Mother and loves her, but not with the kind of love I envision for a marriage. Father accepts Mother as she is, is often annoyed, but says as little as possible, because he knows the sacrifices Mother has had to make.

Father doesn't always ask her opinion about the business, about other matters about people, about all kinds of things. He doesn't tell her everything, because he knows she's far too emotional, far too critical, and often far too biased. Father's not in love. He kisses her the way he kisses us. He never holds her up as an example, because he can't. He looks at her teasingly, or mockingly, but never lovingly.

It may be that Mother's great sacrifice has made her harsh and disagreeable toward those around her, but it's guaranteed to take her even farther from the path of love, to arouse even less admiration, and one day Father is bound to realize that while, on the outside, she has never demanded his total love, on the inside, she has slowly but surely been crumbling away. She loves him more than anyone, and it's hard to see this kind of love not being returned.

So should I actually feel more sympathy for Mother? Should I help her? And Father? -- I can't, I'm always imagining another Mother. I just can't. -- How could I? She hasn't told me anything, and I've never asked her. What do we know of one another's thoughts? I can't talk to her, I can't look lovingly into those cold eyes, I can't. Not ever! -- If she had even one quality an understanding mother is supposed to have, gentleness or friendliness or patience or something, I'd keep trying to get closer to her. But as for

> loving this insensitive person, this mocking creature—it's
> becoming more and more impossible every day!

Any criticism here of Otto the husband and father is limited. This passage is far more an indictment of Edith the wife and mother. To say Edith knew she "would never be first in her husband's affections" could be seen as an indirect criticism of Otto, but it is nowhere near as fierce as what appears to be Anne's direct condemnation of her mother. Likewise "it's hard to see this kind of love not being returned" is a phrase that could be seen as an indirect criticism of Otto, but the passage gives numerous reasons why Otto was justified in withholding his love for his wife, all of them due to Edith's deplorable character.

Two possible motivations emerge for why someone presented these five missing pages as late as 1998. First, Otto wrote them and gave them to Suijk in order to deflect the attention Revisionists were giving to the Diary, suspecting that Otto was the real author. Would Otto ever write anything in the Diary that would condemn himself? And yet, most of the five pages condemn Edith, something consistent with the rest of the Diary. Perhaps the five pages contain enough indirect condemnation of Otto himself for him to have written them in order to deflect any claims that Otto was the real author of the Diary.

Secondly: What possible motive would Meyer Levin have for withholding the five pages? Obviously none, as we have seen. Presumably they were part of the original diaries, which Otto had in his possession, but possibly written by Levin. It would have been Otto's choice to withhold the five pages, not Levin's. Perhaps Otto resented Levin depicting Otto's marriage so harshly, and withheld the pages to maintain his own reputation and to spite Levin. Or perhaps Otto knew Levin's depiction of his marriage was true, and withheld them out of embarrassment. Additionally, Levin may have written such a condemnation of Otto and his wife and marriage to insult and challenge Otto.

The same critique and analysis we have applied to the rest of the Diary applies to the mysterious five pages. They are too mature in writing style and insight to have been written by a teenage girl (especially one said to be rather average); Anne is not likely to have known such intimate details of Otto's life and Otto should not have told her he loved another woman than her mother; a significant profit motive was attached to their presentation; and Otto had multiple conflicting motives for with-holding them until after his and his second wife's death.

Two More Mysterious Pages!

Incredibly, in searching for the five pages, I came across an account of two more missing pages that surfaced in 2018. AFH claims "The covered pages were photographed during a regular check on the condition of the diaries of Anne Frank in 2016".[15] Yet the content of these "covered pages" was not presented to the world until 15 May 2018. Why the two-year delay?

AFH calls this revelation "hidden text on two pages covered up with gummed paper in the first diary of Anne Frank, with its red checked cover". Apparently, "thanks to image processing technology the text could be deciphered". Are we to believe the technology did not exist in 2016 when the covered pages were photographed, but was invented by 2018 when the content was revealed? This is hardly credible.

Nowhere have I ever heard that any of the original pages of Anne's first diary were "covered up with brown gummed paper". If such a thing were in the original diary, someone would have remarked on it long before 2018. Also, someone would have used simple technology such as shining a light through the covered pages to read the text. They would not have had to wait until 2018 for some advanced technology to "decipher" the mystery of the covered pages.

AFH provides a 3:30 minute video depicting the deciphering, with narration in Dutch, but a setting that provides English sub-titles. The imagery clearly shows nothing more than a bright light shining through a page of the diary, with a camera mounted opposite the light. Subsequent imagery shows the photographed pages displaying text processed with

---

[15] New text from diary of Anne Frank revealed," Anne Frank House; www.annefrank.org/en/about-us/news-and-press/news/2018/5/15/new-texts-diary-anne-frank-revealed/

various techniques such as a red light, in order to reveal the text more clearly. It looked to me as if the original photographs were sufficient to read the text without any advanced technology applied. Indeed, at 1:27-1:30 of the video, the hidden pages with their brown paper covering are displayed, numbered 78 and 79 on the surface. Presumably someone added the page numbers after the diary was written. Or was Anne supposed to have added the page numbers? Did Anne number any of the other pages? I have neither heard nor seen that she did.

At any rate, even as displayed in the AFH video, the text can be glimpsed through the brown paper covering, though perhaps not clearly enough to be read. The brown paper does not entirely cover the edges of the pages, and some of the underlying writing is clearly seen beyond the brown paper. Therefore anyone who looked even casually through the diary would know at once that two whole pages were covered with text.

Are we asked to believe that, over the course of 76 years, such otherwise hidden content of one of the most iconic documents in world history was never investigated? Is it possible that the world was never even told that two of the pages were obscured by brown paper? Would not the intense curiosity over what the pages said and why Anne presumably covered them drive investigators to apply a simple light technique to read them, and tell the rest of us? I find it simply unbelievable that the content of two supposedly covered pages was only revealed in 2018.

What do the uncovered two pages say? They contain perhaps the filthiest pornographic smut of the entire Diary. Suzuki has already mentioned some of the Diary's over-sexualized content (recall chapter three), but the uncovered pages are even more excessively pornographic. I am tempted to think these pages were withheld out of shame and embarrassment, but I rather think those who promote the Diary are shameless. More likely they present the uncovered pages to sensationalize and draw more attention to the Diary, and possibly to normalize a more degrading, perverting cultural standard for all children, youth, and adults today.

AFH's web story, "New texts from diary of Anne Frank revealed" states, "The texts that have now been revealed are included in the academic research into the diaries of Anne Frank and her development as a writer..." The only other statement regarding the contents is a quotation by Ronald Leopold, AFH executive director: "Given the great public and academic interest we have decided...to publish these texts and share them with the world. They bring us even closer to the girl and the writer Anne Frank." Tellingly, not a word of the actual content is provided, nor any link to such content.

The video embedded on the AFH page warns at the beginning and end, in both Dutch and English, that it could be a violation of law to post or publish the contents of the uncovered pages. Is AFH trying to suppress knowledge of the content?

Fortunately, I was able to find references to the content elsewhere. Two days after the AFH announcement, the Georgia Commission on the Holocaust posted its own announcement on 17 May 2018.[16] Here we learn: "The text was written on September 28, 1942, and includes five crossed-out phrases, four 'dirty' jokes, and 33 lines about sex education and prostitution." Truly! Immediately the Georgia Commission presents the following statement from AFH (which, ironically, I could not find on AFH's site itself):

> The covered pages do not alter our image of Anne. She regularly recorded 'dirty' jokes or dealt with sexuality in her diary. Over the decades Anne has grown to become the worldwide symbol of the Holocaust, and Anne the girl has increasingly faded into the background. These—literally—uncovered texts bring the inquisitive and in many respects precocious teenager back into the foreground.

This is a blatant attempt to control our reaction to the shocking news that the content is pornographic. It is nothing new for Anne, we are told. Besides, she's become not really an actual girl, but a symbol now, and this new content re-personalizes her as "inquisitive" and "precocious". To any reasonable person, however, it degrades her as perverted and grotesque.

---

[16] Georgia Commission on the Holocaust, "Hidden pages in Anne Frank's diary revealed," May 17 2018;
www.holocaust.georgia.gov/blog-post/2018-05-17/hidden-pages-anne-franks-diary-revealed

The Georgia Commission on the Holocaust provides a link to a "series of frequently asked questions," which goes to the AFH site again, where no FAQs can be found, except questions on how to buy tickets to the "museum," arrange presentations, acquire educational materials and such. I was disappointed, because I have many questions about the uncovered content, in particular, what it actually says.

Once again, I found some of it elsewhere. The Biography website actually displays some of the verbatim content. In its article "The Secret Pages of Anne Frank's diary",[17] which it attributes to "the famed documentarian of Nazi oppression," we see the literal content at last:

> I'll use this spoiled page to write down 'dirty' jokes.

Nothing in the video on the AFH site showing the uncovered pages indicates the original pages were "spoiled" in any way. No marks or soiling or crumpling of the pages can be seen. Why does Anne say the page is "spoiled"? Perhaps she wrote over pages that had other writing on them, which she calls "spoiled"? The AFH analysis of the pages does not indicate this, however. We can see no way in which the pages are "spoiled".

> Do you know why the German girls of the armed forces are
> in the Netherlands? As a mattress for the soldiers.

This is anti-German war propaganda. It is also hypocritical for a sex-obsessed girl to criticize other women for their sexual behavior. It is also racist, attributing degraded sexual habits to German girls only, excluding the sexual habits of Jews.

> A man comes home at night and notices that another man
> shared the bed with his wife that evening. He searches the
> whole house, and finally also looks in the bedroom closet.
> There is a totally naked man, and when that one man asked

[17] Biography, "The Secret Pages of Anne Frank's diary," 11 June 2020; www.biography.com/news/anne-frank-diary-secret-pages

what the other was doing there, the man in the closet answered: 'You can believe it or not but I am waiting for the
tram.'

Thus, infidelity in marriage is thought to be funny to a girl whose own
father confided to her that he loved a woman other than her mother. I
find it beyond belief that so much of the diary of a young girl could be
devoted to sex, even "dirty" jokes hardly suitable for adults.

Referring to a girl's first period, the uncovered pages call it "a sign
that she is ripe to have relations with a man..." This need not be the only
meaning of the sign, and many rites of passage ceremonies consider it a
sign that a girl has become an adult woman. Ripeness for "relations with
a man" need not be the foremost meaning of female adulthood, but it is
to the author of the diaries.

> I sometimes imagine that someone might come to me and
> ask me to inform him about sexual matters. How would I
> go about it? ... [R]hythmical movements [and] internal
> medicament...

Why would Anne imagine someone would ask a thirteen-year-old girl
advice about "sexual matters"? It is inconceivable, unless the inquirer
was a sexual pervert and criminal child molester, or the author was far
older and more experienced than Anne was at the time.

> All men, if they are normal, go with women, women like
> that accost them on the street and then they go together. In
> Paris they have big houses for that. Papa has been there.

Where? Paris, or the whorehouses? Why in the world would Otto tell his
thirteen-year-old or younger daughter about whorehouses in Paris?
Would Anne have no knowledge of whorehouses in the Netherlands
where she lived? Why didn't Otto tell her about whorehouses in the vicinity of his offices in the Netherlands? I have nothing but questions
about this statement.

All this content, incidentally, is dated 28 September 1942 in the diary.

This is the extent of content from the uncovered two pages we are offered by Biography. In the end, we are treated to another quote from Ronald Leopold: "They bring us even closer to the girl and the writer Anne Frank." To my sensibilities, they repulse us away from the degenerate, perverse girl-child, or whoever truly wrote the Diary. It seems to me that Biography and AFH are trying to influence our reaction to such content as healthy and normal, when if not exposed to their suggestions we would naturally see it as filthy and vile, especially in a thirteen-year-old girl. Of course, it is quite possible that the uncovered pages were written by a middle-aged Jewish man after the war, and possibly long after.

Also, the handwriting we can see in the AFH video appears quite different than the rest of the diaries' writing. The uncovered pages look to be written mostly in clumsy block letters, not the orderly cursive style of much of the rest of the diaries. The top area of one uncovered page is indeed written in the orderly cursive writing of the rest of the diaries, with three full lines of the cursive text and parts of two other lines scratched out with some kind of blackish coloring, perhaps the same kind of ink or pencil used to write the rest of the uncovered pages. The rest of the page is in the jumbled block letters.

Have the uncovered pages been subject to the same handwriting analysis as the rest of the diaries? Has a forensic analysis been done on the brown paper and glue used to cover the pages, and the ink or pencil used to write them, in order to determine if they were in existence in 1942 when Anne supposedly wrote and then covered the pages? For that matter, when exactly did Anne supposedly cover the pages, right away after writing them in 1942, or later in 1944 during one of her "edits"? Has any effort been made to discover the content of the scratched-out text? The scratching-out process appears to have been exceedingly thorough and dense, but surely modern technology can determine what was written beneath.

I have seen no mention that any of these standard document analyses have been performed on the uncovered pages. This should be standard procedure for such important historical documents as the diaries, especially when allegedly new material is found and declared. The results should be made prominent and easily accessible. None of the sources I have studied, including AFH, make any mention of forensic, handwriting, or any other analyses for authentication.

The five "missing" pages and the two "hidden" pages are at least as suspect as the rest of the diary, and indeed more so.

The Ballpoint Pen Claim

Some Anne Frank Diary revisionists claim significant portions of the diaries were written in ballpoint pen, a device that was not in widespread use until 1950. This alone would prove the diary was a fraud. For instance, in "The Anne Frank diary Fraud" by Brian Harring, featured on TBR News.org,, Harring states, "When Anne allegedly rewrote the diaries, she used a ball point pen, which did not exist in 1945". The Harring account further states,

> The results of tests, performed at the BKA laboratories, showed that 'significant' portions of the work, especially the fourth volume, were written with a ballpoint pen. Since ballpoint pens were not available before 1951, the BKA concluded those sections must have been added subsequently.

Harring concludes:

> In the end, BKA clearly determined that none of the diary handwriting matched known examples of Anne's handwriting. The German magazine, *Der Spiegel*, published an account of this report alleging that (a) some editing postdated 1951; (b) an earlier expert had held that all the writing in the journal was by the same hand; and thus (c) the entire diary was a postwar fake.[18]

---

[18] Brian Harring, "The Anne Frank diary Fraud," TBR News www.whale.to/b/harring.html

The great British historian and expert on document fraud David Irving commented on the ballpoint pen issue in a letter to a young woman inquirer. Irving wrote:

> (After Irving requested that Otto Frank submit the diaries to forensic analysis,) Frank again refused to let the diary out of his grasp, whereupon the West German police sent two trained forensic laboratory experts with their equipment all the way down to Switzerland to examine the documents in situ. Their conclusion shocked the world, although for propaganda reasons the impact has been far less than it would have been in other circumstances. Parts of the diary, the detectives found, had been written in ball-point ink.

Similar to other Revisionists, Irving came to the same conclusion:

> The earlier Lübeck Judgment had been based in part on a graphologist's sworn statement that the diary had been written throughout by one and the same hand! If so, it followed that therefore it had all been written in the 1950s or later, long after Anne's death. Otto Frank subsequently claimed that the diary was not, after all, all in the same hand, and admitted that it had been embellished by others, hence the ball-point ink.[19]

The Anne Frank House presents this issue differently than such revisionists as Harring, but consistent with Irving's statement that Frank admitted embellishment. Under a section titled "Are there really entries in the diary in ballpoint pen?," AFH states:

> The origin of the 'ballpoint myth' is the four-page report that the Federal Criminal Police Office (the *Bundeskrimi-*

---

[19] David Irving, Letter to Sarah Jules, February 15, 1986, London; www.fpp.co.uk/Auschwitz/docs/controversies/AnneFrank/Jules150286.html

nalamt or BKA) in Wiesbaden, which was published in 1980 (sic). In this investigation into the types of paper and ink used in the diary of Anne Frank it is stated that 'ball-point corrections' had been made on some loose sheets. The BKA's task was to report on all the texts found among the diaries of Anne Frank, and therefore also on the annotations that were made in Anne's manuscripts after the war.[20]

Further:

However, the Dutch investigation by the Forensic Institute in the mid-1980's shows that writing in ballpoint is only found on two loose pages of annotations, and that these annotations are of no significance for the actual content of the diary. They were clearly placed between the other pages later. The researchers of the Forensic Institute also concluded that the handwriting on these two annotation sheets differs from the writing in the diary 'to a far-reaching degree.' Photos of these loose annotation sheets are included in the NIOD's publication (see *The Diary of Anne Frank: The Revised Critical Edition*, 2003, pages 168 and 170).

Below are images of the two pages in the RCE. Both show diary sheets with attached ballpoint notes. AFH even presents the name of the person who wrote these two pages in ballpoint ink: "Mrs. Ockelmann was a member of the team that carried out the graphological investigation into the writings of Anne Frank around 1960."

---

[20] The Authenticity of the diary of Anne Frank," Anne Frank House; www.annefrank.org/en/anne-frank/go-in-depth/authenticity-diary-anne-frank

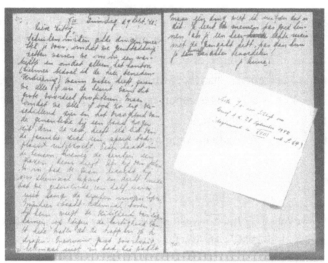

RCE, p. 168

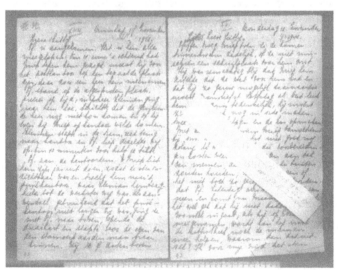

RCE, p. 170

In this case, the AFH is most likely correct. Some revisionists have exaggerated the ballpoint pen analysis and failed to identify which pages were written in ballpoint pen and by whom they were written. I have not been able to find a copy of the original BKA document nor the Forensic Institute document, but if AFH is being honest and the handwriting of the ballpoint pen pages is different from the rest of the diary, then its assertion that these pages were inserted later by a "graphological researcher," who AFH identifies as "Mrs. Ockelmann," is most likely accurate.

If, on the other hand, AFH is being fully honest it would provide files or links to the original documents regarding the ballpoint pen analyses, and would display the two ballpoint ink pages on its webpage devoted to the issue—but does not.

The likelihood that some revisionists have unfairly represented the ballpoint pen issue does not mean all other analyses of revisionists are also incorrect. Each must be based on its own merits and not dismissed simply because one claim was inaccurate. Also, ascribing hostile or "anti-Semitic" motives, by "extreme right-wing" people, to the ballpoint pen debate is disingenuous of AFH. It cannot know motive, and many revisionists are motivated primarily by a desire for historical accuracy and validity. Many would not consider themselves "extreme right-wing" either, whatever this label is thought to mean. AFH provides no definition.

Conclusion

It appears as if AFH's denunciation of revisionists with derogatory terms and ascribing to them hostile motives reveals its own agenda: holocaust promotion through perpetuation of the Anne Frank diary myth. This supports its income and reason for existence, perpetuates the view of Jews as innocent victims and Germans as evil "Nazis," suppresses and distorts knowledge of National Socialism, justifies the existence of the nation of Israel, and continues to frighten Jews into either living in or supporting Zionist Israel.

Diary promoters at AFH call it "one of the most read, most important and most inspiring books in the world." Other diary promoters use similar hyperbolic language. Biography.com calls Anne Frank "the famed documentarian of Nazi oppression." They exaggerate the impact of the story of Anne Frank because they have an agenda to promote, namely the Holocaust horror story, for which the pathos of the diary contents falsely wins many hearts and minds over to the Jews-as-victims, "Nazis"-as-monsters depiction.

That so much real-world influence relies on a document—The Diary of Anne Frank—which for many reasons cannot be trusted to be authentic, concerns revisionists. Our main motivation is to correct the historical record and allow whatever adjustments must be made in society, politics, economics, culture, and religion to bring our reality into line with the truth. If Annelies did not write the diary at all, or only wrote a small portion of it, and if someone else, such as Otto Frank or Meyer Levin or both, actually wrote all or most of the Diary, it is not heresy to say so. It would be a betrayal of history and of truth to withhold critical analyses of a document which has so much influence in so many ways. This—the crumbling of their influence—must be a main motivation for why the Anne Frank House continues to defend and promote the Diary, despite its many obvious problems.

Despite it all, revisionists persist in their quest for the truth. Every day, more and more people begin to see behind the charade of lies and deception, and discover honest history.

BIBLIOGRAPHY

Butz, A. 1976/2003. *The Hoax of the Twentieth Century*. Theses and Dissertations Press.

Crowell, S. 2011. *The Gas Chamber of Sherlock Holmes*. Nine-Banded Books.

Dalton, T. 2019. *The Jewish Hand in the World Wars*. Castle Hill.

Dalton, T. 2020. *Debating the Holocaust: A New Look at Both Sides* (4th ed.). Castle Hill.

Faurisson, R. 1978/1982. "Is the Diary of Anne Frank Genuine?" *Journal of Historical Review* 3(2). Available at: www.ihr.org/jhr/v03/v03index.html

Faurisson, R. 1985. *Is the Diary of Anne Frank Genuine?* Institute for Historical Review (Torrance, CA).

Faurisson, R. 2000. "The diary of Anne Frank: Is it genuine? An update." *Journal of Historical Review* 19(6). Available at: www.ihr.org/jhr/v19/v19index.html

Felderer, D. 1978/1979. *Anne Frank's Diary: A Hoax.* Institute for Historical Review (Torrance, CA).

Frank, A. 1948. *Het achterhuis; dagboekbrieven van 12 Juni 1942-1 Augustus 1944*. Contact (Amsterdam).

Frank, A. 1991/2000. *The Diary of a Young Girl: The Definitive Edition*. (O. Frank and M. Pressler, eds.; S. Massotty, trans.). Doubleday.

Mattogno, C. 2016. *Healthcare in Auschwitz*. Castle Hill.

Netherlands Institute for War Documentation. 1986/1989. *The Diary of Anne Frank: The Critical Edition*. (D. Barnouw and G. van der Stroom, eds.). Doubleday.

Netherlands Institute for War Documentation. 2003. *The Diary of Anne Frank: The Revised Critical Edition*. (D. Barnouw and G. van der Stroom, eds.). Doubleday.

Rudolf, G. 2005/2017. *Lectures on the Holocaust* (3rd ed.). Castle Hill.

Schnabel, E. 1958. *Anne Frank: A Portrait in Courage*. Harcourt, Brace.

Sheppard, S. 2001. *Anne Frank's Novel: The Diary is a Fraud* (2nd ed.). Heretical Press.

CPSIA information can be obtained
at www.ICGtesting.com
Printed in the USA
LVHW030525161122
733175LV00001B/52